Unveiling Gratitude

Character, Strength and Virtue

Unveiling Gratitude

Dr Mark Amadi

Paperback Edition First Published in Great Britain in 2020
eBook Edition First Published in Great Britain in 2020

Copyright © Dr Mark Amadi 2020

Dr Mark Amadi has asserted his rights under 'the Copyright Designs and Patents Act 1988' to be identified as the author of this work.

All rights reserved.

No part of this document may be reproduced or transmitted in any form or by any means, electronic, mechanical, photocopying, recording, or otherwise, without prior written permission of the Author.

All scriptural quotations are taken from the
King James Version (KJV).

ISBN: 978-1-913438-10-4

aSys Publishing

Contents

Acknowledgement 1
Foreword 2
Introduction 4
Unveiling Gratitude through the Cross 4
New Nature 4
Spiritual Brokenness 6
Grace – The Person of Christ Jesus 7
Revelation of Grace 8
God's Benevolence 9
Gratitude – Power in Action 11

Chapter One 15
Gratitude, Grace, Glory 15
Spirit of Gratitude 19
Role of Grace in Gratitude 20

Chapter Two 28
Understanding Gratitude 28
    Scope of Gratitude 28
    Revealed Will 29
    Essence of Gratitude 31
Nature of Gratitude: Translational gratitude 32

Chapter Three 39
Mystery of Gratitude 39
Comparative Gratitude 41
Why Be Grateful? 43
To Whom to Be Grateful? 45

Barriers to True Practice of Gratitude 47
Covetousness 48
    Overview of Covetousness 48
    Sin of Covetousness and Its Consequences 49
    Gratitude Overpowers Covetousness 52
Murmuring 53
    Overview of Murmuring 53
    Sin of Murmuring and Its Consequences 53
    Gratitude Overpowers Murmuring 56
Pride 58
    Overview of Pride 58
    Sin of Pride and Its Consequences 59
    Gratitude Overpowers Pride 61

Chapter Four 69
Doctrine and Attitude of Gratitude 69
Attitude of Gratitude 72

Chapter Five 81
Companion Virtue and Potency of Gratitude 81
Humility and Gratitude 82
Contentment and Gratitude 83
Consequences of Discontentment 86
Potency of Gratitude 87
Gratitude – A Healing Balm 89
Purity of Heart 91
Essence of Gratitude 94
Completeness 96

Chapter Six 105
Doxology of Gratitude – In All Things Give Thanks 105
Cultivating Faith and Gratitude 107
Gratitudinal Thankfulness (Luke 17: 11–19) 109

Chapter Seven 122
Gratitude: An Eschatological Reality 122
A Peculiar Eschatological Reality Phenomenon 126
Salvational Grace.. 127
Eschatological Reality of Redemptive Worship (Thanks in Heaven)... 129

Chapter Eight 140
Conclusion... 140
Bibliography... 145
About the Book.. 149
About the Author... 150

Index.. 151

Acknowledgement

First and foremost, I am eternally grateful to God and thank Him for His great plan of salvation. He made this book possible, as I could have never written it without His grace. This book, as a service before God, is written for His glory alone.

I extend special love and thanks to my parents, family and friends who have encouraged me to serve the Lord through this medium. My special thanks to all members of the Fountain of Peace ministries for their encouragement and support. Although it was my intention to list all their names here, I was unable to do so owing to their inexhaustibility.

My thanks also go to Dr Isaac Ojutalayo, Pastor Tunji Odebiyi, Dr Andrew Davies, and many others who were of tremendous help to me.

In addition, I appreciate my little Immanuela and Eliana whose smiles always encourage and inspire me to keep writing.

My deep appreciation goes to Yemi Atanda, for the confidence and hope he instilled in me that all will be well!

I also thank all those who read this book and offered me helpful comments. I am thankful to the editors and designer as well for their services.

Foreword

We live in a world that sometimes appears to be unhappy, irritable and ungrateful. It's perhaps a little hard to argue that life is more pressured and intense for us than it has been for every generation before us – after all, we are not living through the horrors of a world war or anything like that – but it is certainly true that the challenges that confront us as a society and individuals are incredibly complex and have profound implications for our flourishing and indeed our survival. From climate change to childcare costs, global conflicts to social media trolling, trade wars to body image pressures, we just have so much to worry about that it is unsurprising that our mental and physical health and well-being are so often under pressure from stress, anxiety and fear.

It seems to me that Dr Mark Amadi has hit on something of a cure for many of those modern sicknesses in pointing us to the importance of gratitude. It's hard to be jealous, angry, covetous, proud and discontent and be grateful at the same time. Choosing to be grateful dispels such negative and harmful attitudes as rapidly as turning on a light switch dismisses darkness. Being content with and grateful for all the Lord has given us is part of the key to achieving happiness and fulfilment in our lives and becoming women and men of generous heart and spirit. Thankfulness, as Mark shows us, is a choice available to us all, a radical rejection of one-upmanship, consumerism and commercialism, grounded in our response to God's incredible grace exhibited in the gift of his Son, our Lord Jesus Christ.

I can think of no one better than Mark to bring us this reminder. Mark is one of the happiest, most gracious and thankful men I know. I don't think I've ever spoken with him without being encouraged and uplifted. If I had a pound for every time he thanked me, I would be a very rich man indeed! He is a supreme example of the blessings and benefits that flow from living a thankful life and models impeccably the lifestyle he describes in this book.

One of the few things we do here on earth now as well as continue to do in heaven is expressing our thanks, praise and worship to our almighty and eternal Father. We have an eternity to voice that gratitude, so we may as well learn now how to do, and, as Mark shows us so beautifully here, the gratitude that he describes vividly as "the ever-evolving and expanding appreciation of God's grace" will transform our lives in so many ways.

I know this book and this man's ministry will be an immense blessing to you. Don't forget to say thank you to him!

Dr Andrew Davies

Director, Edward Cadbury Centre for the Public Understanding of Religion

University of Birmingham, UK

Introduction

Unveiling Gratitude through the Cross

This book presents a biblical and spiritual perspective on gratitude. It aims to help us understand gratitude from God's viewpoint and unlock the power of gratitude for everyday living. This chapter lays the foundation to the message contained in the book that pertains to grace – accepting and responding to grace – which is Jesus Christ, for unveiling gratitude.

The message contained herein is conceived divinely to enable us to live in gratitude for attaining a level of spiritual maturity and discipline in order to express the divine nature of God as we interact with all His creations, especially *man*, so that we can behold the glory of God, not only by the Word we preach but also through our character, attitude and behaviour. Living a life of divine gratitude can be realised only when we truly accept God's grace and respond to His grace (John 3:36), whose fullness is in Christ Jesus (John 1: 14–17), and His finished work on the Cross for us (Romans 6). Through the Cross, we receive a "new nature," where every argument brought against us is invalidated and every curse is transformed into a blessing. Living in this new nature empowers us to unveil gratitude through a lifestyle rooted and grounded in Christ by the living word of God, confirming Apostle Paul's advice to the Christians of Colossae:

> *Rooted and built up in him, and stablished in the faith, as ye have been taught, abounding therein with thanksgiving.* (Colossians 2: 7)

New Nature

Grace and the finished work of Christ Jesus on the Cross are the foundational concepts of our Christian living today. Through the finished work of Christ on the Cross, our old nature has been crucified, and we are given a new nature (Romans 6). For this reason, we should always give thanks and praise, which is God's will for us (1 Thessalonians 5:18).

> *We can only be of this new nature when we fully accept and respond to God's grace, which comes through our Lord Jesus Christ.* (Galatians 2: 19–20)

Moreover, through the finished work of Christ on the Cross, an eternal river of grace has been released upon us. We enjoy this eternal river of grace only when we are broken and completely surrendered to God. Therefore, let me clarify here that God's grace is not an abstract concept or a thing but a person. Jesus Christ is God's grace personified (Titus 2: 11–15).

God wants us to receive an abundance of grace, as having an abundance of grace is having an abundance of Jesus. Grace is free because the giver has *paid* the cost, and for this reason, our entire life and lifestyle must be of gratitude. God's grace has opened so many doors for us, most of which we have traversed without knowing. Moreover, the grace received demands a response, and God's grace finds its completion when it flows through us to others by our act of expressing gratitude (*Being the light and salt*: Matthew 5: 14–16).

Gratitude, like faith, hope, love and commitment, is not an inborn trait but a pillar that can be strengthened over time by being in Christ to reflect God's image – His likeness – in which we are created (Genesis 1: 26–30). Being created in God's image – His likeness – simply means that we are made to resemble Him. The image of God (*imago dei*) refers to the immaterial part of man and not some bodily, biological form, as God is a spirit (John 4: 24). Here, we are, therefore, talking about the spiritual image of God.

God's image is not anthropomorphic; rather, the term "image" describes humans as "theomorphic" (God-shaped). Although the Scripture describes God as having arms,[1] hands,[2] eyes,[3] ears[4] and wings,[5] these are only metaphors used to convey His ability. God's image here refers to humanity as the royalty appointed by God as His representatives, regents and stewards of His creations.

> On the other hand, being created in His likeness simply means we are made to resemble God or be like God in holiness, character and attitude.

Bearing the truth that we are created in God's likeness in mind is a sufficient reason to be replete with gratitude, regardless of the circumstances in which we find ourselves (1 Thessalonians 5: 18). The practice of gratitude as a spiritual discipline realigns us with God and His will and increases His manifestation in our lives. Therefore, to truly live a life of divine gratitude and genuinely express gratitude, the necessity of being spiritually broken is placed on us, as gratitude is spiritual in nature and a spiritual discipline. It is far more than a feeling but a moral virtue, which Jesus Himself commended (Luke 17: 14–17). Spiritual brokenness precedes divine gratitude, which draws us nearer to God:

> *The Lord is nigh unto them that are of a broken heart; and saveth such as be of a contrite spirit.* (Psalm 34: 18)

Spiritual Brokenness

We, as Christians, are called to continually strive to be like Christ and have the mind of Christ – grow into the image and likeness of God (Romans 8: 29).[6] One of the greatest ways through which we can share Christ's life and express our gratitude to God is proclaiming God's goodness and bringing others into God's presence by living a lifestyle of gratitude. A significant part of responding to God's grace is sharing the Good News of God's grace and love with all by expressing gratitude. Evidently, gratitude is not just an emotion we choose to express in response to grace or some good favour but a spiritual act of brokenness that emits a sweet aroma (*Christlike character*), like the one from the Alabaster jar (Mark 14: 3–9). Gratitude does not respond to situations but to the resurrected Christ who dwells inside us, which empowers us to live out the life of Christ Jesus (Galatians 2: 20).

Grace – The Person of Christ Jesus

Therefore, accepting grace makes us actually see who we are in Christ and not from the physical dimension of man and his circumstances. Grace is the person of Christ Jesus being made readily available to all who accept and respond to it. God's dealing with me has enabled me to understand that grace is neither a constellation of rules to be followed nor a form of catalyst to propel self-effort or desire. Instead, Grace is a person, living His life through you.[7] Living under grace is being joined together and sharing one's life with Christ (Galatians 2: 20–21, see also 2 Corinthians 4: 10–11).

Sharing the life of Christ (Romans 8: 1–17) gives us access to everything willed to us by God (John 3: 16, Ephesians 1). It means being united with Christ, and this involves dying to the flesh (Romans 6). Having this life of Christ and assurance of God's heavenly blessing, we ought to live a life of gratitude that is purely a gift from God by grace. Every good and perfect gift is from God (James 1: 17, see also 1 Corinthians 1: 4). Gratitude cannot be appreciated unless grace is understood divinely. In this regard, Philip Yancey states as follows:

> Grace means there is nothing I can do to make God love me more and nothing I can do to make God love me less. It means that I, even I who deserve the opposite, am invited to take my place at the table in God's family.[8]

Put in context, Yancey's thought expresses that grace is God's unconditional love for us. Ephesians 2: 1–10 seeks to explain that grace is God's unconditional love in action to save us. At this stage, it is important to clearly understand that God did not extend grace to us because of who we are but because of who He is: *The Lord God Almighty.*⁹ The grace of God is freely enfolded in the love of God that gives us what we do not merit and deserve. The revelation of grace needs to be well understood to truly express or unveil gratitude through our lifestyle.

Revelation of Grace

The grace of God is so amazing and powerful that it empowers us in our weaknesses, even in our inadequacies and the calamities of life. Growing up has made me realise that when we do not have the natural abilities within our own mental and emotional make-up to do the great things or carry out God's divine assignments, accepting God's Grace will qualify us to do those extraordinary things that God intends for us. In essence, Christianity cannot be properly understood without an adequate knowledge and revelation of grace. Grace is not a theology or a subject matter but a person, whose name is Jesus. John 1: 14 and Titus 2: 11–14 give an enhanced spiritual meaning to the place of grace in the person of Christ:

> *And the Word was made flesh, and dwelt among us, (and we beheld his glory, the glory as of the only begotten of the Father) full of grace and truth. (John 1:14). 11 For the grace of God that bringeth salvation hath appeared to all men, 12 Teaching us that, denying ungodliness and worldly lusts, we should live soberly, righteously, and godly, in this present world; 13 Looking for that blessed hope, and the glorious appearing of the great God and our Saviour Jesus Christ; 14 Who gave himself for us, that he might redeem us from all iniquity, and purify unto himself a peculiar people, zealous of good works.* (Titus 2: 11–14)

The above verses explicate that Jesus Christ is God's grace personified. John begins his gospel by explaining that Jesus is the eternal Word of God who came physically and set up His earthly tent among us so that grace could abound for us to live a fruitful and dominion life. This is the mandate given to us at the beginning of creation in Genesis 1: 26–28. Because of such benevolence from God, we owe Him nothing but gratitude because of the grace that has reconnected us back to purpose.

God's Benevolence

From my modest experience of Christian living and the walk with God, I have learnt that it is imperative to understand and recognise that a tremendous working power (from God) is essential if the ministry of the gospel is to prosper where people are being converted and lives being transformed. This power is nothing less than God Himself through Christ Jesus (2 Corinthians 4: 7).

In other words, we need the power of God flowing through and operating in us to achieve any real success in the Lord. Without God's divine power and ability (grace) flowing through and operating in us, it will be difficult to ascend to the top of the mountain that He calls us to climb. This power comes to us fully and truly when we respond to grace with a heart of gratitude – the residing power of God in us by abiding in Him and Him in us (John 15).

Gratitude humbles us to appreciate the finished work of the Cross. To be precise, gratitude is the overflow of the thanksgiving of a humble heart (Colossians 2: 7).

> My growth in ministry has only been by the mercy and grace of God, for His glory and glory alone. After receiving such privilege or, in better words, grace, I remain grateful to God who has called me.

The expression of grace and gratitude has become my lifestyle. I have come to the understanding that the working of grace in my life is what has made me who I am. When we sincerely accept and respond to grace, it evokes gratitude. Grace and gratitude work together. Our embodied act of gratitude enables others to encounter God as well. God is a God who requires or deserves gratitude. If so, could there be a "doctrine of gratitude"?

God being a God of gratitude implies that gratitude is a doctrine. Doctrine means teaching. The doctrine of gratitude stands on the foundation of giving thanks to the Lord according to His righteousness and nothing less (Psalm 7: 17). God in the Old Testament is shown to be a God of gratitude in that He always expected the Children of Israel to show gratitude for His wonders. For example, after crossing the Red Sea, despite beholding such a great wonder, they grumbled like some of us today. The consequence of this was that their journey in the wilderness was prolonged and they were bitten by fiery serpents (Numbers 21: 5–10).

Each time we forget the Lord's goodness, He gets angry because He is a God of gratitude (1 Samuel 12: 9, Psalm 78: 11, Psalm 106: 13). As God taught the Israelites to be of gratitude, likewise Jesus taught His disciples to be of gratitude (Luke 17: 17). The apostle Paul emphasised that it is God's will for us to live a life of gratitude (1 Thessalonians 5: 18).

An essential ingredient in showing gratitude is remembering what God has done for us. He takes gratitude so seriously that Moses had to warn the Children of Israel:

> *Then it shall be, if you by any means forget the Lord your God, and follow other gods, and serve them and worship them, I testify against you this day that you shall surely perish. 20 As the nations which the Lord destroys before you, so you shall perish, because you would not be obedient to the voice of the Lord your God.* (Deuteronomy 8: 19–20; Cf. Leviticus 26).

God does not want us to *forget* His benevolence. He wants us to express gratitude by living His life, living the life He desires for us[10] so that others may see Him through us. Our act of gratitude is both an expression of spiritual life and the capacity for divine blessing. This means gratitude is a mystery for encountering God's exceeding greatness.

Gratitude – Power in Action

The mystery of gratitude is that all we need have been provided through Christ who sacrificed His life so that we may truly live. Gratitude is a mystery because it entails following the leadership of God the Father, God the Son and God the Holy Spirit when situations make no sense to man, like in the case of Daniel (Daniel 3 and 6). Gratitude must be in place for the glory of God to manifest in our lives. Jesus understood the mystery of gratitude and applied it throughout His ministry on earth to release blessings and perform healings and great wonders. Lacking the revelation and understanding of the mystery of gratitude sometimes makes us waste time on spiritual exercises that produce no result. Jesus made use of this mystery to unlock many miracles in uncompromising situations (Luke 9: 16, John 6: 11, John 11: 41, 1 Corinthians 11: 24).

Gratitude is the ingredient required for the activation and manifestation of the other mysteries of the Kingdom.

> *Sometimes, our situation is not the primary will of God for us but our response to the situation, which Paul stressed that in all situations, give thanks to God.* (1 Thessalonian 5: 18)
>
> *Fulfilling this mystery brings God's Kingdom into our heart; let thy Kingdom come.* (Matthew 6: 10)

One of the mysteries that controls the other mysteries of the Kingdom is gratitude. Increase and influence, deliverance and healing are controlled by the mystery of gratitude. Walking in the mystery of gratitude empowers us to tackle all the trials of life victoriously. A key mystery that has been consistently demonstrated in the Scriptures is that ingratitude hands you over to your enemies (See Deuteronomy 28: 47–48)

As I have faced many trials and tribulations in life and have been saved by grace and grace alone, my intention here is to unveil divine gratitude and, at the same time, seek to explain that gratitude is a doctrine that should be taught and practised. Practicing gratitude is the beginning of appreciating and responding to grace through the sanctification works of Christ Jesus on the Cross (Titus 3: 8), which is the *will* of God (1 Thessalonians 5: 18).

When we uphold the truth of God, we gear towards gratitude, but when we suppress God's truth by the act of wickedness (Psalm 10: 2–11), ingratitude is born (Romans 1: 18). For example, the Israelite nation did what they "deemed-fit" (Judges 21: 25) because their backsliding was rooted in ingratitude:

> *So the children of Israel did evil in the sight of the Lord. They forgot the Lord their God and served the Baals and Asherahs.* (Judges 3: 7)

Each time God punished the Israelites, it was because they lacked a heart of gratitude and for not upholding His righteousness and truth. Gratitude is more than just waving our hands in the air to say, "Thank you, Lord."

A heart of gratitude (thanksgiving, praise, worship, gratefulness) is directed towards God, and gratitude overflows the banks of the heart like a river. Therefore, standing and being rooted in the Word of God and His truth accord us the capacity to truly overflow with the attitude of gratitude despite our circumstances.

> Looking back and seeing how gracious God's grace has transformed me, for His glory, gratitude has become my garment and turban. I am proud to say I am a full-blown product of grace.

In other words, gratitude is power in action, springing from within, not only as a way of life but also as a soul-winning tool to sustain ourselves in Christ as well as to convert and transform others and situations. When gratitude and grace meet, light is created for others to see God (Matthew 5: 13–16).

As we unveil gratitude, may God give us the revelation in His knowledge to understand and witness how wonderfully made we are so that we can continually live a life of gratitude. Nevertheless, on a more personal note, worshipping in truth pertains to the Word of God circulating in our consciousness, providing a greater and deeper spiritual and physical capacity for the mental attitude of gratitude:

> *That you may walk worthy of the Lord, fully pleasing Him, being fruitful in every good work and increasing in the knowledge of God.* (Colossians 1: 10)

As this book is indeed about unveiling gratitude, I will biblically explain what divine gratitude is, what it involves and what its eschatological reality of redemptive worship (thanks in heaven) is, for a proper understanding so that we do not fall short of this essential *will* of God. Therefore, to unveil gratitude, let's begin by examining the biblical connection between gratitude, grace and glory.

Dr Mark Amadi

Endnotes

1 Deuteronomy 33: 27, Psalm 89: 10, Psalm 98: 1, Isaiah 63: 12, Acts 13: 17

2 Isaiah 59: 1, Psalm 98: 1, Isaiah 66: 2, Psalm 8: 3, Psalm 19: 1, Isaiah 64: 8, 1 Chronicles 29: 12, Acts 13: 11

3 Genesis 6: 8, Psalm 32: 8, Psalm 33: 18, Job 34: 21, Proverbs 15: 3, 1 Peter 3: 12

4 Isaiah 55: 3

5 Psalm 91: 4, Psalm 17: 8, Jeremiah 49: 22

6 Here, let me clarify that God's plan and purpose in creation and redemption is to have a family – the redeemed conform to the image of His Son.

7 Galatians 2: 20 – "I am crucified with Christ: nevertheless I live; yet not I, but Christ liveth in me: and the life which I now live in the flesh I live by the faith of the Son of God, who loved me, and gave himself for me."

8 Philip Yancey, What's So Amazing About Grace; Revised ed. (Zondervan; Grand Rapids, MI, 2008), p. 74. Also see Denise George, Tilling the Soul: Prayer Penetrates Your Pain Revised ed. (Zondervan; Colorado Springs, CO, 2005), p. 79.

9 Psalm 106: 8 – "Nevertheless he saved them for his name's sake, that he might make his mighty power to be known." See also John 3: 15–18

10 Living a life that exalts God – finding out who we are in Christ and living out this truth daily, doing His will (Ephesians 4:1).

Chapter One

Gratitude, Grace, Glory

Our joy in the Lord, our maturity in Christ Jesus and the activation of our spiritual blessings are characterised by gratitude exceeding a one-time experience for us to live a lifestyle of continuous gratitude and grace.[1] When grace is appreciated, gratitude is born naturally. In other words, when grace is appreciated, gratitude becomes a habitual, daily lifestyle, which is God's will for us (1 Thessalonians 5: 18). Everything around us speaks of the amazing grace of God for our comforts and security. Hence, there exists a need to be grateful, as through Christ Jesus, grace has been spread out for continuous victory.

There are unseen things as well as seen things (2 Corinthians 4: 18), and what we focus on can affect how grace is appreciated. A huge difference exists between them: unseen things are eternal; seen things are temporal. When hope is built on the unseen, eternal joy is established, producing a life of gratitude. Therefore, to appreciate God's grace for living a life of gratitude, we need to look away from the seen things, ceasing to seek a future of worldly advantages or fearing the present of distresses. Focusing on the unseen as we live in Christ Jesus gives us the hope to live in joy and thankfulness. According to Paul, grace has been spread out for us to abound in God's glory, regardless of the seen things (troubles or pleasures):

> *For all things are for your sakes, that the abundant grace might through the thanksgiving of many redound to the glory of God. (2 Corinthians 4:15)*

The above verse highlights three powerful and interconnected "Gs" – grace, gratitude (translated as thanksgiving in the text) and glory. A review of the original text written in Greek gives a better understanding of the relationship between grace and gratitude. "Thanks" in Greek is linked to the term "grace" (Charis), which becomes "Eucharistian" (gratitude) when expressed. This means the terms "grace" and "gratitude" (translated as thanksgiving in 2 Corinthians 4: 15) have the same root in Greek.

Jesus has been recorded using a similar word while celebrating the Last Supper:

> ...And he took bread, and when he had given thanks [εὐχαριστήσας – eucharistēsas] he broke it and gave it to them. (Luke 22: 18–19).

Therefore, paraphrasing 2 Corinthians 4: 15 in its original form reads as follows:

> It is all for your sake so that as grace extends to multitudes of people, it may increase gratitude to the glory of God.

In essence, grace and gratitude have a direct relationship; when grace increases, gratitude also ought to increase. The combination of grace and gratitude creates light in our lives, reflecting God's presence and, at the same time, giving glory to God (Matthew 5: 13–16). Manifesting God's glory through our lifestyle is to appreciate the power of grace, which is linked to God's glory, as God does all things for His glory[2] and will never share His glory.[3] God's glory is shared when His grace is not appreciated and we attribute the received power, success and intellect to self-effort. When Ananias and Sapphira in Acts 5 as well as Herod in Acts 12 decided to share God's glory by "lying"[4] and being arrogant[5] respectively, they died. God used this as an example of or warning about the consequences of coveting a share of His glory. The lack of gratitude is a gateway to further terrible sins.

Unveiling Gratitude

> Being grateful is accepting and responding to the magnanimity of God's blessings and accomplished works. As we appreciate and practise God's accomplished works, we get to know Him, not just as a providential God but as a God of gratitude.

God's greatest goal for us is to glorify Him. The purpose of glorifying Him is not really to increase the beauty of His perfections or fill some void in Him but to display His glory through our lifestyle for His praise[6] by being full of gratitude for the received grace. Thus, gratitude is an attitude of continuous thanksgiving. God is a God of Gratitude. God's mercy and goodness, which endure forever, are indications that He deserves not a one-time thanksgiving but a continuous one.[7] The goodness of God is His nature or character to deal generously and benevolently with us in every circumstance. He loves us so dearly and wants us to live in continuous thanksgiving, as He has surrounded us with His goodness and mercy. For this reason, He made it a way of life, and He expects us to live it by being grateful or thankful in all circumstances.[8]

The works and wonders of God go far beyond the intellect and power of human reasoning or imagination. Therefore, to behold and express God's glory, the gratitude for His grace must be paramount, which requires the brokenness of our heart. God's glory has a purpose: to reveal or manifest His glory in us so that we can become a reflection of His glory, His power, His presence and His essence. Therefore, understanding this interrelationship is important, as it helps unveil the true meaning of gratitude.

Let me expressively say here that gratitude is beyond mere actions (actions of self-will or power). As gratitude is a feeling associated with a response to grace, the expression of gratitude is, therefore, an unequivocal expression of humility and encouragement about what we have. David, whose life was associated with grace, embodied such an attitude. He expressed gratitude in whatever season he found himself and always had the perspective of gratitude, expressed in praise.[9] To be of gratitude (praise) like David, three aspects are essential: brokenness[10], trust (Psalm 18)[11] and expression (1 Chronicles 29: 10–13). These aspects empower us to live a God-centred life, marked by the fruit of the Holy Spirit (Galatians 5: 22), emerging from the workings of the Holy Spirit dwelling in us.

Knowing and doing God's will involve discarding our opinions and prejudice for His.

In other words, gratitude is the recognition of the gratuitous extension of God's love and friendship[12] to us through His Grace so that we can live out His "image" – His likeness (Genesis 1: 26–29). This explains that gratitude involves more than just uttering the words "thank you." In recognising the intention of God's grace, we are obliged to live in His *will* in order to appreciate His grace given to us freely as a gift. David's lifestyle reveals the three conditions required to be of gratitude: recognising God's intention of choosing him (David), being appreciative and thankful for the grace given and reciprocating the grace by living out God's will – to be a gift to others in order to receive salvation.[13]

Gratitude is best unveiled or expressed when we fulfil God's purpose for our lives – affecting and influencing others by living God's will.

What we sometimes interpret as gratitude is sometimes not, especially in connection with eternity, which focuses on unseen things (2 Corinthians 4: 18). For example, social etiquette stipulates that we express verbal appreciation for help rendered or favours received; these are seen things.[14] However, saying "thank you" or similar complimentary words does not in itself signify gratitude. Gratitude is spiritual; it is the equivalent of feeling and abiding by the presence and grace of God to express His likeness of love and goodness.[15] It is beyond audible verbal expressions and visible actions emanating from human will.

Spirit of Gratitude

The spirit or heart of gratitude is born of the Spirit of God. It is a fruit of God's Spirit displayed by those living and walking in unbroken fellowship with the Spirit of God (Galatians 5: 22–26, Matthew 5: 1–11). Gratitude is a spiritual attribute conveyed through the workings of the Holy Spirit that dwells within us. The spirit of gratitude increases the grace upon us and empowers us to radiate God's glory in our daily lives.

Gratitude cannot be expressed or "willed into existence" if it is does not already exist within us. It is not an ephemeral feeling of happiness that varies and is based on prevailing circumstances or conditions. Gratitude arises uncoerced from the innermost part of the heart when the outer (carnal) man has been broken by the Holy Spirit.

> While gratitude is an inward recognition of appreciation, thanksgiving is an outward mien of gratitude.

The breaking of the outer man is the only way for our spirit (inward man) to be liberated in order to release gratitude. The outer man cannot obey God's rules; hence, abiding by God's demands will be impossible:

> *The carnal mind is enmity against God: for it is not subject to the law of God, neither indeed can be. (Romans 8: 7)*

The only work God approves is that of the reborn spirit. Many of us are fundamentally unfit to express gratitude because we still live according to the flesh (outer man/carnal mind) and our inward man has not been strengthened by the Holy Spirit (Ephesians 3:16). When we surrender to God and the Lord Jesus Christ, the Spirit of Christ will work within us to break the outer man (self-will and the lustful desires of the flesh) and strengthen our inward man to unveil true gratitude.

> Gratitude is more than an ephemeral feeling of happiness or a collection of words of appreciation. True gratitude is spiritual and can only surface after the breaking of the "outer man" by the Holy Spirit.

Role of Grace in Gratitude

True gratitude is a response to grace, and it flourishes in the realm of grace. Our hearts must be in a constant state of gratitude towards God for His grace, as His grace has made everything available for us:

Every good gift and every perfect gift is from above, and cometh down from the Father of lights, with whom is no variableness, neither shadow of turning. (James 1: 17)

Our lives and blessings are gifts from God. He is the giver of every good and perfect gift, and gratitude should be our response to His prodigal grace towards us. Having this constant awareness of God's grace keeps our inner man in a state of gratitude, which invariably radiates outwards and becomes visibly perceived by those around us.

Expressing gratitude requires knowledge, not the knowledge that makes us inflate, but the knowledge that makes us realise we are nothing without the grace of God. This realisation should keep us humble and desirous to remain connected to Jesus Christ (Colossians 3: 3–4). As He is the head, and we are the parts of His spiritual body, without His grace, we can do nothing (John 15: 5–7). Gratitude helps us to *keep ourselves connected* to Him, *increase the grace* upon us and empower ourselves to *radiate His glory* in our daily lives.

God's grace towards us does not change, as it is a divine enablement by the life of Christ in us to be what God has called us to be[16] – a royal priesthood (1 Peter 2: 9–10) at the acceptance and response to grace. Though, sometimes, our feeling towards God's grace may waver either because of fear or sin,[17] which also affect the sense of gratitude. In the divinity of God's grace, grace cannot change for a moment but can be abused, about which Paul warns that we should renew constantly our spiritual vitality so as not to fall short of the grace of God.[18] The Bible doesn't reference any instance when God's grace has ceased even for a moment, even during the "400 years" of God's silence between Malachi and Matthew.[19] Rather the Bible records occasions when the heart of God's people deviated[20] from Him, attracted punishment and, not to say, His grace ceased, for example, when the Philistine captured the Ark of Covenant (1 Samuel 5). Consequently, as God's grace does not waver even for a moment, our encounter and experience of the enjoyment of God's grace can change either because of the lack of gratitude or the abuse of grace.

> Gratitude understands grace as a gift for daily living, empowering a grateful heart to focus and maximising the grace they have in the form of the seemingly little and not what is lacking.

When grace is appreciated, our hearts swell in gratitude. Marvelling at God's amazing grace prompts us to be more thankful for God's amazing grace, causing us to realise we need His grace moment by moment. Grace reveals our helplessness and unveils our understanding to depart from sin – to recognise and accept God's will – for living a life of gratitude. When grace is unveiled, gratitude is expressed because grace reveals where God has picked us from, how He has cleansed us and the hope of glory we have in Christ Jesus.[21]

Gratitude and grace humble us to unlock and receive more grace and, thus, forever live in exceeding gratitude without sin (James 4: 6). Gratitude, the power to appreciate and acknowledge what we have or have been given, is not a gift but an attribute of godliness, a Christian lifestyle embedded in the "value of grace," a spiritual discipline we develop to live the life God expects of us. Gratitude through grace is not merely concerned with the performance of outward acts, observances or ceremonies of gratitude, as said earlier, but gratitude, an act of godliness, is fostering a real inner spiritual relationship with God.

When gratitude is enacted by grace, gratitude becomes genuine and vivacious, not synthetic or artificial.[22] One who lives a life of gratitude is attentive to God's presence and the power of His might, obedient to His Word and motivated by both love and deep reverence for Him.

Gratitude, being rooted in the appreciation of grace, brings blessings to our life as well the lives of all those with whom we associate. It is a potent instrument to achieve God's purpose,[23] as it opens our heart and eyes to see His goodness that surrounds us. In other words, gratitude rejoices in what was and what is, to make the best of the seemingly nothing, leaving no room for regret, regression and revenge.

> Gratitude is a gem that is precious, peaceful, powerful, provocative and progressive: the more we are grateful, the more we see the reason to be grateful, as gratitude is the lens that reveals God's incredible grace at work in our lives when we think God is silent.

In conclusion, gratitude is primarily both a spiritual weapon and a spiritual act of worship. While it is commendable to physically express appreciation through words, gifts or deeds, such actions are empty and meaningless if they lack sincerity and truthfulness from the heart. What qualifies our words and actions as acts of gratitude is the genuine appreciation that emanates from the spirit after the breaking of the outer man. To truly express gratitude, the flesh must die so that pure worship can emerge from our spirit to glorify the Lord in our acts and expressions of gratitude. Until the outer man is broken, the inner man cannot

Unveiling Gratitude

produce "the anointing ointment of worship – the spirit of gratitude" (John 12: 3). Gratitude is not just a social etiquette; rather, it is a divine truth (spiritual mystery) that needs to be unveiled to gain a proper understanding of its true essence, forms, purpose and nature, as we live our lives in Christ Jesus.

As the feeling of gratitude is usually an honest reciprocation from our hearts when grace (unmerited or unjustifiable favour) is received, the expression of gratitude (thanks) will communicate humility, godliness. Therefore, gratitude is not simply the virtue of responding to perceived grace but the virtue by which we both recognise and respond to God's grace that leads us ultimately to God through Jesus Christ as we move from grace to grace. Our grateful response, the act of thanksgiving, is also a form of praise and worship,[24] a lifestyle prescribed by God (1 Thessalonians 5: 18).

An understanding of gratitude, grace and glory will help us unveil the mystery of gratitude. Gratitude is a spiritual mystery that can only be unveiled by God Himself when our heart is reconciled in Him. Gratitude is a mystery to the "unbroken" because true gratitude goes beyond the mindfulness of the sensations of gratitude. The manifestation of gratitude as a physical sensation at a bodily level to a spiritual level is comprehensible when the true meaning of gratitude is unveiled through the lens of God. One mystery behind growing from grace to grace to reflect God's likeness and behold His glory and wonders in unfavourable circumstances is gratitude.

> Gratitude is a power that turns the unfavourable into favourable when not only felt but expressed.

For gratitude to not remain a mystery, we need to possess a proper and an in-depth understanding of gratitude from God's perspective. In other words, the way to secure assured understanding about the mystery of gratitude is to have our heart knit together in the love of God and love others with a heart of appreciation.

How can we understand gratitude?

Endnotes

1 D. Elton Trueblood, (Nashville, TN: Broadman, 1982), p. 18.

2 According to the Bible, God does everything for His own glory. God created everything through Himself and for Himself (Colossians 1: 16). He created the world to declare His glory (Psalm 19: 1–4) and made man in His likeness for His glory (Isaiah 43: 7). He condemns all who dishonour His name for His glory (Exodus 20: 7) and also saves us to bring glory to His name (Jeremiah 14: 7, Psalm 25: 11).

3 Isaiah 42: 8

4 Acts 5 – Ananias and Sapphira lied to the Holy Spirit. They allowed the spirit of greed rather than the spirit of gratitude to possess them. They had the grace of giving to God but shared the glory of God's grace to be a partaker of the extension of His grace to the Church for their selfish reasons. Gratitude is to be given back to God for everything we have received.

5 Acts 12 – Out of arrogance, Herod didn't give glory to God, which led to his death. The lack of gratitude can cause spiritual death. Herod was filled with pride and vanity, which emptied him of gratitude. Arrogance is a terrible sin that leads to spiritual death. Our genuine acceptance and response to grace empowers us to ascribe to God the praise due to Him and Him only (1 Chronicles 16: 29, Psalm 29). Only a heart of gratitude can give glory to God.

6 Isaiah 48: 9–11

7 Psalm 107: 1 – "Oh, give thanks to the Lord, for He is good! For His [a]mercy endures forever." See Ephesians 5: 20

8 1 Thessalonians 5: 16–18 – "16 Rejoice evermore. 17 Pray without ceasing. 18 In everything, give thanks, for this is the will of God in Christ Jesus concerning you."

9 David, the man after God's heart, expressed his gratitude by singing many of his songs as prayers to the Lord, for example, Psalm 57.

10 Emptiness of self. Without emptiness, appreciating the grace that will empower us to live a life of gratitude is challenging. Brokenness is important in our Christian journey, as it gives way for the supernatural to be revealed.

11 Trust here means running to God as well as depending on and trusting Him. David made God his refuge, always running to God for help, and was sincere and diligent about it. See Psalm 46. God can be found – Jeremiah 29: 13.

12 God's love and friendship are wrapped in grace and have been extended to all who hear and obey Him (John 3: 15–17). This grace has been before human existence in God's only begotten Son, Jesus (John 1: 1–5).

13 Matthew 5: 13–16 – This is the reward for reciprocating grace. Reciprocating grace empowers to live God's intended life, to be the Light and Salt of the earth. Also see David S. Dockery & David E. Garland, Seeking the Kingdom (Wheaton: Harold Shaw, 1992), pp. 35–37.

14 2 Corinthians 4: 18 – True gratitude doesn't come from the temporal. Sometimes, the seen becomes a veil separating the flesh from beholding grace and the set glory, which will cause a response for gratitude.

15 Genesis 1: 31 – God saw all that He had made and called it "very good." This means God is a god of gratitude. Gratitude is

a divine character that stems from the almighty God Himself (Psalm 107: 1).

16 Titus 2: 11–12 – Paul is simply saying that the *grace* of God is given to train and empower us to reject sin and live godly lives. Succinctly put, grace has set us free from sin to the contrary, but we must accept grace, respond to it and be of gratitude to live out the life of Christ imputed in us through His death and resurrection.

17 Romans 6: 1–2 – Likewise, Jude warned that it is possible to "change the grace of our God into a license for immorality" (Jude 4). See and compare Jude 4 with Romans 5: 20

18 Hebrews 12: 12–16 – "Looking carefully lest anyone fall short of the grace of God; lest any root of bitterness springing up cause trouble, and by this many become defiled."

19 The 400 years of silence refers to the time between the Old Testament and New Testament, during which God did not speak to the Jewish people (Malachi 4: 5–6). God's apparent silence over the 400 years was not because He was absent or inactive but because only those with the eyes of faith could see Him and His workings. It is not that He wasn't active during these years; He was. Only a heart of gratitude (faith) can empower us to do the greater works of God when others think He is silent (Compare Hebrews 11: 6 and Hebrews 12: 14).

20 Deviate here refers to acts of disobedience (1 Samuel, Psalm 99).

21 1 Timothy 1: 12–17

22 Synthetic or artificial here means hypocritical. Gratitude is not hypocritical but a matter of the heart, truthfulness and purity. It is not just honouring with lip or eye service but possessing a pure heart through the righteousness of Christ (Matthew

5: 8, Romans 4: 3–5), as God looks at the heart (1 Samuel 16: 7, see Matthew 15: 8, Isaiah 29: 13, Mark 7: 6).

23 Living a lifestyle of gratitude to God is one of the most effective spiritual weapons that has the potential to bring forth God's richest divine blessings in our lives. Living a life of gratitude is for our own blessings and joyfulness.

24 Thanksgiving, an expression of gratitude, is an act of praise culminating in acts of worship as we recognise and respond to the grace of God. See Carmichael, Liz. Friendship: Interpreting Christian love (London: T & T Clark International, 2004).

Chapter Two

Understanding Gratitude

Scope of Gratitude

Gratitude is a popular concept in the Positive Psychology Program. However, Christian gratitude, Christ-shaped gratitude, has a different connotation regarding the practice of gratitude. The act of gratitude is God's will for us, as evident in Paul's instruction to the Thessalonian Church:

> *Rejoice evermore, pray without ceasing. In everything give thanks: for this is the will of God in Christ Jesus concerning you." (1 Thessalonians 5: 16–18)*

From a Biblical view, gratitude is a lifestyle that emanates from God's presence dwelling in us. His presence in us enables us to express godliness (God) through our behaviour, attitude or character. In other words, gratitude should be evoked by or dependent on not only our numerous acquisitions or emotions but also the greater awareness of God's presence, His goodness and His purpose.

Gratitude manifests in various forms. It can manifest as an emotion, an attitude, a personality trait or a coping mechanism in times of adversity. In the biblical context, gratitude is a spiritual virtue – an act of worship (Exodus 20: 3–11, John 4: 24, Revelation 4: 11). It entails appreciating God's faithfulness and marvellous works with a pure heart, regardless of circumstances. A true state of gratitude is not conditional on receiving any form of blessings, honour or recognition but the overflow of godliness from a humble heart being broken by Christ who dwells in us (Matthew 5: 5).

> Gratitude is an inwardly generated response, an expression of the appreciation of God's given privileges; His mercy, grace and faithfulness that are ever present to get us through in times of trouble.

Gratitude provides access to supernatural flourishing and lifting. The Scriptures clarify that the righteous who engages in gratitude as a lifestyle shall flourish like a palm tree (Psalm 92: 12). Gratitude is one of the vital forces that attracts God's blessings into our lives. Jesus was of gratitude when He prayed over the five loaves of bread and three fish for heavenly intervention, which brought about an overflow and the glorification of God. The purpose of every act of gratitude should be to give glory to God. Until our act of gratitude brings glory to God, we will not experience His supernatural fruitfulness. When our gratitude gives glory to God, He commits and does the extraordinary. Gratitude can be expressed in different forms, but in whichever form, it must bring glory to God and be a lifestyle, as such is the revealed will of God for His people.

Revealed Will

God's revealed will for us is to live a life centred on *joy, prayer* and *thanksgiving (gratitude)*. It is important to note the nature of the adverbs describing the three actions (verbs) of *rejoice, pray and give thanks* stated in 1 Thessalonians 5: 16–18. The three adverbs – *always* (to describe "rejoice"), *without ceasing* (to describe "pray"), *in everything* (to describe "give thanks") – all depict *a continuous, perpetual state of being*, not just a temporal or situational practice.

This implies that gratitude should be our constant, unshifting state of being even as we navigate through the vicissitudes of life. Having this perspective will give us strength when storms hit, hope when betrayed and peace when all else fails. This disposition is aptly captured in the following hymn:

> *When peace, like a river, attendeth my way, When sorrows like sea billows roll, Whatever my lot, thou (God) hast taught me to say: "It is well; it is well with my soul."[1] – Horatio G. Spafford*

The hymn by Spafford explains that gratitude is a powerful weapon to be employed in order to remain in God's will for us – to be faithful and thankful in all situations.[2] It suggests that gratitude takes our eyes off ourselves, our problems, to focus on God in times of trouble. The expression "It is well" emphasises that a heart of gratitude leaves no room for complaints and doubts but only appreciation. Thus, the admission "It is well" means that regardless of our circumstances, our soul is 100% well because we are surrounded by God's goodness and mercy and His promise that He will not leave us alone.[3]

Although I precisely don't know the workings of the Shunammite woman's mind when she uttered, "It is well," but from her answer, I understand that she was not thinking but thanking God with the faith and hope that her promised son will not "just die." Such is the attitude God wants from us when we face the trials and tribulations of life. The Shunammite woman, despite the death of her son, still confessed that "It is well."[4] She kept her faith even through hard circumstances. Even when all the circumstances around her looked grim, she still said, "It is well." This unveiled her heart of gratitude that believed that God would never fail her. She held onto the faith that the God who gave her the child was also very capable of reviving the child, and this is how God wants us to behave when we are faced with challenging situations. Gratitude empowers us to recount the glorious works God has done in our lives, and this gives us hope, confidence and internal peace that He will do even more as seen in the case of the Shunammite woman who had faith.

Regardless of what we encounter in life, the peace we gain through Christ Jesus gives us a sense of assurance to tell ourselves, "It is well with my soul." Jesus gave us the assurance and encouraged us that our hearts should not be troubled.[5] With this blessed assurance and encouragement from Jesus, we must always be grateful at all times in whatever circumstances,[6] as Jesus, the "Fourth Man,"[7] is with us.

Therefore, a grateful heart rooted in Christ Jesus can remain joyful, faithful, prayerful and thankful amidst all trials and tribulations of life. To better understand this kind of uncommon gratitude, we will briefly examine its essence and nature.

Essence of Gratitude

Regardless of the form gratitude takes, its essence is to reveal God's nature in us as we respond in appreciation to His love and diverse grace. Thomas Merton in his book *Thoughts in Solitude* puts as follows:

> To be grateful is to recognize the love of God in everything He has given us – and He has given us everything. Every breath we draw is a gift of His love, every moment of existence is a grace, for it brings with it immense graces from Him. Gratitude therefore takes nothing for granted, is never unresponsive, and is constantly awakening to new wonders and to the praise of God's goodness. For the grateful person knows that God is good, not by hearsay but by experience. And that is what makes all the difference.[8]

The above quote explains that the essence of gratitude is to recognise and appreciate the love of God in everything and acknowledge that all we are or have has been graciously given to us by Him.

Nature of Gratitude: Translational gratitude

True gratitude is *translational* in nature. Translational simply means relating to translating or changing into another form. In the biblical context, it refers to the transformation of our lifestyle into one that is characterised by God's fundamental nature of love, displayed in acts of gratitude.

The invisible God is always seeking avenues to express His nature in our visible world. For example, Jesus being made flesh to dwell amongst men was a translational process where the divine, invisible, eternal God took the form of man to fulfil the plan of salvation and redemption of mankind (John 1:1–14, John 3:15–18).

In the same vein, Jesus, while on earth, instructed that we let our light shine before men so that they may see our good works (on earth) and glorify our Father (God) in heaven (Mathew 5: 16). Gratitude must be translational in character to be unveiled.

> Translational gratitude is, therefore, the principle of translating the invisible God's fundamental nature of love into visible acts of gratitude in our daily interactions, transactions and relationships with the rest of God's creation.

Translational gratitude shares the same attributes as the love of God. Therefore, to understand the nature of translational gratitude, we ought to reflect on the nature of God's love. God's love for us is not bound by preconditions, prejudices or prerequisites. We did not do anything to earn or deserve God's love, the Bible says, "*but God demonstrates His own love toward us, in that while we were still sinners, Christ died for us*" (Romans 5: 8). God has shown Himself to be LOVE so that we do not fall short of eternal joy, unless we sway away from His love.

God loved us before we loved Him (1 John 4: 19). He loved us despite our fallen state, mistakes and weaknesses. He did not wait for us to clean up our acts or be grateful to Him before loving us.

He loved us not because of who we were but in spite of who we were; such is the nature of God's love for us.

Similarly, translational gratitude is not based on reciprocity – "giving good, to get good." Like God's love, it is endowed regardless of the recipient's disposition towards the giver. Not only should we show gratitude towards people for their acts of kindness, but also should our gratitude be considered as a vehicle for conveying God's love to all – the good or bad, the deserving or undeserving, the sinful or holy. Even seemingly insignificant or mundane tasks done by others on our behalf should be warmly appreciated with a heart of gratitude.

Without a heart of gratitude, bearing with the weaknesses of others and covering their flaws with love are impossible (Genesis 9: 22–26, Romans 15: 1). God Himself demonstrated this in the Garden of Eden when He made a garment of skin (from an animal) to cover the nakedness of Adam and Eve after their fall (Genesis 3: 21).

In His eternal plan of redemption, God gave His only begotten Son (Jesus Christ) as a "once-and-for-all" sacrifice to restore us back to Him (Hebrews 10: 10); this ultimate act of sacrificial love revealed how appreciative He was of His creation (John 3: 16 – 18).

Choosing to bear the weaknesses of others should not be viewed as condoning sin; rather, it should be considered an expression of love from a grateful heart that realises we all were once sinners and we all are still susceptible to sin at any time but for the grace of God.

> A heart of gratitude is a heart of love, loving unconditionally, radically demonstrating our love for God, which is expressed in our relationships with others. If we do not love, expressing gratitude to the visible man, how can we then express gratitude to the invincible and invisible God?

Although we express our gratitude towards men, what we are really doing when we do so is worshiping God through those acts of gratitude. Others deserving, acknowledging or appreciating our gratitude is insignificant, as gratitude in its purest form is an unadulterated spiritual worship offered to the invisible God, regarding which Jesus cautioned as follows:

> *Take heed that you do not do your charitable deeds before men, to be seen by them. Otherwise you have no reward from your Father (God) in heaven...your Father who sees in secret will Himself reward you openly. (Mathew 6:1-4)*

When we display the love of Jesus Christ with our lifestyle, we offer a spiritual form of worship that glorifies Him and draws men to God. This is the kind of worship that God seeks. God does not want to be an abstract, distant, unrelatable Being; rather, He seeks to be an intricate part of our daily lives on earth and wants to work wonders through us for the glory of His name. Jesus unequivocally states that true worship is not about performing religious rites in designated centres of worship:

> *...the hour is coming when you will neither on this mountain, nor in Jerusalem, worship the Father...the true worshipers will worship the Father in spirit and truth; for the Father is seeking such to worship Him. (John 4: 21–25)*

In summary, gratitude is not just an emotion; rather, it is an attribute of God, a divine nature. Translational gratitude, therefore, brings the touch of divinity to humanity. It connects the supernatural nature of the invisible God to the natural needs of man in a practical, relatable manner. Practising a lifestyle of translational gratitude reflects the nature of God. It reveals the God in whom we believe to the world around us without the need for sermonising or reciting Scriptures (2 Corinthians 3: 1–6). Thereby, our lives become "living epistles" that people read to see and know God.

Unveiling Gratitude

Gratitude is far more than our vocal expressions or expressional gestures, especially when we receive something good. The Scripture says we should give thanks in all circumstances, good or bad, as such is the *will* of God for us.[9]

The interpretation of what is bad to man does not have the same connotation as what is bad to God. What looks bad in the sight of man can be the breaking into the dawn of God's glory (Isaiah 58: 8). From God or human's perfective, how then do we interpret "bad"? Were the Shunammite woman and Job's circumstances bad ones? From the human perspective, it could really be bad. However, from God's point of view, it was a situation of "glory," as He was showcasing His might and glory in those circumstances. Let me point out here that till our eyes are enlightened to see God's wonderous working, our circumstances shall remain a mystery to us, which we sometimes subjectively interpret. Therefore, Apostle Paul prayed that our eyes be opened because of divine revelation.[10]

The attitude of gratitude, being thankful for everything that happens to you, opens your eyes to see the greatness before you, empowering you to know that every step forward is a step towards achieving great and glorious things than your current situation.

Then what will foster a spirit of thanksgiving within us when life seems to be ridden with discouragement, disappointment, depression, disease, dejection and devourers and nothing around you and within you seems encouraging, energising, elevating or empowering, and yet you are commanded to be thankful, expressing gratitude? It takes nothing but the grace of God through Christ Jesus. This means gratitude is a force or an urge beyond human emotion; it is spiritual in nature and a mystery that needs to be understood through the lens of God so that we can find ourselves in God's *will*. It is only the broken man who can be thankful in all circumstances, as this involves faith,[11] obedience[12] and humility[13] in the Spirit of Christ Jesus.

> Realising God is in control of every circumstance of ours, good or bad, and being thankful are fuelled by the Spirit through a broken heart that can see Christ seated in the storm, having an understanding of God's perfect will for the circumstance.

Emphasising the *will* of the Father, Jesus explained that it not about preaching, prophesying, healing, casting out demons and performing good and wonderful works but doing the Father's *will* that qualifies us to enter God's Kingdom (Matthew 7: 21–23).[14] Examining 1 Thessalonians 5: 18 reveals that gratitude is God's *will* for us. Is it optional? How can we be thankful when our walls are falling? Is gratitude then a mystery?

Endnotes

1 Horatio Gates Spafford (1873).

2 1 Thessalonians 5: 18 – In everything, give thanks; for this is the will of God in Christ Jesus for you.

3 Hebrews 13: 5 – Let your conduct be without covetousness; be content with such things as you have. For He Himself has said, "I will never leave you nor forsake you."

4 2 Kings 4: 8–37

5 John 14: 27

6 Ephesians 5: 20 – "Giving thanks always for all things to God, the Father, in the name of our Lord Jesus Christ."

7 Daniel 3: 25 – "Look!" he answered, "I see four men loose, walking in the midst of the fire; and they are not hurt, and the form of the fourth is like the[a] Son of God."

8 Thomas Merton, Thoughts in Solitude, 33 (1956).

9 1 Thessalonians 5: 18 – "In everything give thanks: for this is the will of God in Christ Jesus concerning you."

10 Ephesians 1: 16–20 – "16 Do not cease to give thanks for you, making mention of you in my prayers: 17 that the God of our Lord Jesus Christ, the Father of glory, may give to you the spirit of wisdom and revelation in the knowledge of Him, 18 the eyes of your [a]understanding being enlightened; that you may know what is the hope of His calling, what are the riches of the glory of His inheritance in the saints, 19 and what is the exceeding greatness of His power toward us who believe, according to the working of His mighty power 20 which He worked in Christ when He raised Him from the dead and seated Him at His right hand in the heavenly places, 21 far above all principality [b] and

[c] power and [d] might and dominion, and every name that is named, not only in this age but also in that which is to come."

11 Hebrews 11: 6 – "But without faith it is impossible to please him: for he that cometh to God must believe that he is, and that he is a rewarder of them that diligently seek him."

12 1 Samuel 15: 22 – "And Samuel said, 'Hath the Lord as great delight in burnt offerings and sacrifices, as in obeying the voice of the Lord? Behold, to obey is better than sacrifice, and to hearken than the fat of rams'." Our good will, wonderful works and evens services to God become ordinary sacrifice when lacking obedience to God's will. Gratitude is born from a heart of obedience and not sacrifice. For sacrifice to be meaningful and acceptable, it must obedience centred and oriented.

13 Matthew 5: 5 – "Blessed are the meek: for they shall inherit the earth." See Psalm 37: 11 – "But the meek shall inherit the earth and shall delight themselves in the abundance of peace." "Blessed" in this verse can also be translated as "happy." The blessedness is from God's perspective and not human's perspective of happiness. It is spiritual prosperity, joy, victory and wealth, not necessarily earthly happiness. Thus, gratitude is spiritual and living in the joyfulness of the Lord, and that is when you can be thankful in all circumstances, as God Himself is the circumstance. The earth is the Lord's and its fullness (Psalm 24), and if so, no circumstance is greater than Him. Every circumstance to showcase God's mercy, grace and power to the unwise, jubilating the heart and lives of the righteous who trust in Him.

14 Matthew 7: 21–23 – "21 Not everyone that saith unto me, Lord, Lord, shall enter into the kingdom of heaven; but he that doeth the will of my Father which is in heaven. 22 Many will say to me in that day, Lord, Lord, have we not prophesied in thy name? and in thy name have cast out devils? and in thy name done many wonderful works? 23 And then will I profess unto them, I never knew you: depart from me, ye that work iniquity."

Chapter Three

Mystery of Gratitude

> *But we speak the wisdom of God in a mystery, the hidden wisdom which God ordained before the ages for our glory… Now we have received, not the spirit of the world, but the Spirit who is from God, that we might know the things that have been freely given to us by God. (1 Corinthians 2: 7, 12)*

Mystery is something unclear to, unknown to or not yet comprehended by man. Colossians 1: 26 defines a mystery as that "which hath been hid from ages and from generations, but now is made to manifest to his saints." Gratitude is a mystery because not all understand its foundation and the reason to rejoice and be thankful in difficult circumstances. It takes a heart of understanding to comprehend God's mystery, and when understood, it is no longer a mystery but a revelation.

Mystery does not refer to truths that are difficult to comprehend, rather to truths that can only be understood by divine revelation (God).[1] All operations of the Kingdom are mysteries, and engaging in the mysteries of the Kingdom makes us acquire mastery over (and become a master of) such mysteries to fulfil God's purposes. Gratitude is a mystery of the Kingdom, which when clear and understood, empowers us to live the life expected of us by God through Christ Jesus (1 Thessalonians 5: 18).

> Gratitude without pure obedience, humility and understanding is spiritual blindness to God's likeness and colour and practice.

God topples mysteries and does not retain mysteries for the sake of them. He never withholds but always gives or reveals His truth to those who accept Him (John 3: 15–18, Luke 8: 10). In Paul's days, God's act of accepting and loving the Gentiles like the Jews was a mystery His people couldn't understand, and they wondered why God should love the Gentiles.[2] Likewise, godly gratitude is yet a mystery to many today regarding why they should be thankful amidst calamity.[3]

Notwithstanding, the Kingdom of God operates on mysteries,[4] and to understand, engage and achieve the results of the Kingdom, the mystery of our faith must be held and rooted in obedience[5] for expressing gratitude. Unveiling gratitude is understanding the mystery of gratitude so that we don't fall short of God's grace to behold and enjoy the blessings of the Kingdom, which are made known to only those who respond to grace.

The things of God are mysterious to the natural man; they can only be discerned spiritually, as revealed by God's Spirit. Man's intellect and cleverness cannot unravel the things of God; they will remain a mystery to him. Paul, therefore, states in 1 Corinthians 2: 12 that we have been given the Spirit of God to know the things of God.

Many of us struggle in our walk with God because we try to interpret God's words with our human intellect. Consequently, we fail to capture the spiritual significance of His instructions and are unable to understand or do His will.

Having a myriad of academic qualifications, a high intelligence quotient or exceptional oratory eloquence does not qualify one to handle the things of God. In fact, oftentimes, God will choose the "weak and foolish things" of the world to shame the wise. We, therefore, must learn to empty ourselves of what we know and approach God in humility so that He can fill us with His wisdom and give us true revelation by His Spirit.

Thus, an attitude of gratefulness results as an expression of the awareness of God's benevolence and faithful provision towards us, which Thomas à Kempis describes as follows:

> Be thankful for the smallest blessing, and you will deserve to receive greater. Value the least gifts no less than the greatest and simple graces as special favors. If you remember the dignity of the Giver, no gift will seem small or mean, for nothing can be valueless that is given by the most high God.[6]

Being appreciative of and thankful for tangible or intangible gifts can be a gateway for receiving exceeding greatness from God. Gratitude in its spiritual formation completes a circle that begins with the grace of God, reaching out to humans through the finished work of Christ Jesus on the Cross, and humans reciprocally responding or giving a gift back to God by living a holy lifestyle in thanksgiving – praise, worship and/or service. False liberty or humility of mind and presumptuous self-confidence are formidable deterrents to the practice of true gratitude and heavenly visitations. God is prodigal and has extravagantly given us the grace of comfort and blessings, but man's wickedness is revealed when he is unable to return all to God with gratitude. Being grounded, rooted and established in God and giving God all glory for everything great and wonderful things received, which ultimately come from God alone, keep us from being proud (John 5: 44). In view of this, living in gratitude is God's revealed will for us:

> In everything give thanks; for this is the will of God in Christ Jesus for you.[7]

However, different perspectives exist on gratitude today, giving way to what I call comparative gratitude.

Comparative Gratitude

Over the years, research has provided fascinating evidence of the benefits of gratitude, and numerous studies have explored dispositional gratitude and reliably revealed that gratitude is a trait that is positively related to happiness and well-being as well as that improves sleep and stress management.[8] Furthermore, different perspectives exist on gratitude today, and a considerable amount of literature has been written on the subject. Some researchers describe gratitude as an element of positive psychology, while others view gratitude as a cyclical spiritual force (karma).

> The highest expression of our gratitude is not in the sweetness of fine uttered words but the living of those sweet uttered words.

The proponents of *positive psychology*[9] describe gratitude as a perpetuator of happiness. It is viewed as a good health practice that improves the physical well-being of the practitioner. Positive psychology also teaches gratitude as an instrument for fostering peace within one's self and in one's community. Gratitude interventions and studies are progressively emerging in applied psychology settings with the potential role of gratitude as a resilience factor, for example, in educational environments, work-related contexts and health and clinical psychology arenas.[10]

The science of gratitude propounds that being grateful is a good attribute for a happy life and encourages us to have a "grateful personality." The findings from a study published by the American Psychological Association[11] reveal that possessing a grateful personality is correlated with increased life satisfaction, happiness, optimism, hope and decreased anxiety/depression. The study also submits that practices such as keeping diaries, daily reminders and intentional moments of thankful reflection enhance happiness and give a sense of meaning to life.

Similarly, many eastern religions teach about the spiritual dimension of gratitude. It is labelled as "good karma" – a principle of cause and effect where the intents and actions of an individual (cause) influence the future of the individual (effect). In such religions, gratitude is believed to operate in a cycle as a universal spiritual force, which when released, attracts blessings back to the individual releasing the force.[12]

Given the various ideologies on gratitude today, understanding the biblical concept of gratitude is critical for believers in the Lord Jesus Christ seeking to live a life of gratitude in line with God's will. Three fundamental questions are pertinent as one ponders this matter: *(i) Why should I be grateful? (ii) To whom should I be grateful? (iii) How can I practise true gratitude?* A biblical perspective on each of these questions is provided in the rest of the chapter.

Why Be Grateful?

Although we may find ourselves in challenging economic and health situations or unfriendly circumstances, numerous reasons still exist to be grateful. The adage "count your blessings" means to be grateful despite one's assumed predicament (1 Thessalonians 5: 16–18). However, we may encounter times when counting our blessings can be difficult. We should not wait for something outstanding to happen to us or wait for Thanksgiving Day in order to feel grateful and express gratitude. Gratefulness[13] is always a humbling experience and involves giving thanks for everything in life.

> Significatively, gratefulness is the highest form of thought that breaks the natural man, allowing the spirit of gratitude to cause an overflow of joy that brightens our day and makes us a light – a source of joy and hope – producing faith in others to live on.

In the current postmodern or consumerist society, we tend to emphasise what we lack or what other people have that we do not. Whereas in essence, gratitude is the feeling of appreciation for what we already have.

Although positive psychology teaches us to show appreciation for the benefits received, gratitude does not need a trigger or positive occurrence to be expressed. It springs from the joy of the Lord overflowing in our hearts and is completely independent of the events occurring around us – whether good or bad. This form of gratitude is a fruit of the Holy Spirit (Galatians 5: 22); it is not and cannot be produced by natural man, regardless of how intellectual or morally virtuous he is.

In life, we may encounter times when it seems there is nothing for which to be grateful. Sometimes, our best laid plans don't pan out the way we envisage, leaving us feeling stuck and hopeless. Nevertheless, we need to be grateful, even when we feel nothing good is happening to us.

As believers in Jesus Christ, we should rest in the knowledge that God orchestrates all things behind the scenes and makes it work together for our good, just as He has said He will. Though we may not always understand what God is doing, it does not mean He is wrong or He has abandoned us.

God demands that we trust in Him completely and rest in His strength. A walk with God is a walk of faith:

> *But without faith it is impossible to please him: for he that cometh to God must believe that he is, and that he is a rewarder of them that diligently seek him. (Hebrews 11:6)*

Failing to believe that God is loving, faithful and ever-caring can make us ungrateful and impatient. Whenever we seek help outside of Jesus Christ (God's will) or try to do things our way, such endeavours will always lead to fruitlessness, especially regarding God's will and purpose for us (Deuteronomy 28, Proverb 14:12, Psalm 1, Psalm 46: 10).

God, the Father of our Lord Jesus Christ, is omniscient (all-knowing); we, on the other hand, are limited in what we know. I have learnt from various experiences in life and ministry that there are many things we do not know at present that will only become clearer with the passing of time. If God were to give us a glimpse into tomorrow, then we would bow our head in worship and appreciation, just like Job (Job 1, Job 6). Having faced different trials, including the loss of his children as well as the deterioration of his marriage, health and wealth, Job eventually got a glimpse of the omniscient God and humbly declared as follows:

> *I have heard of thee by the hearing of the ear: but now mine eye seeth thee. Wherefore I abhor myself, and repent in dust and ashes. (Job 42: 5–6)*

At the end of Job's trials, God restored all that he had lost in multiple folds. As believers in Jesus Christ, we have a relationship with God based on a far better covenant than that of Job. Christ in us is the hope of glory; therefore, regardless of the challenges faced, we have hope because we know that in all things God has us covered. His promise to us as follows:

> *I will never leave you nor forsake you. (Deuteronomy 31: 6, Hebrews 13: 5)*

However, we must remember that a lifestyle of gratitude does not make us immune to calamities, rejection, pain or sorrow (Matthew 27: 29–31). Therefore, we should not wait for things to be right before we express gratitude. Every occurrence in our life (whether good or bad) should serve to bring us into a deeper revelation of who God is.

To Whom to Be Grateful?

Only those who have touched God's throne of grace in grateful worship can show true gratitude towards others. The Scripture records two occasions where human lips have touched Jesus Christ: when a woman kissed Jesus' feet in worship (*kiss of gratitude* – Luke 7: 36–47) and when Judas Iscariot kissed Him on the cheek (*kiss of betrayal* – Matthew, 26: 48, Mark 14: 44, Luke

22: 48). Both kisses are significant in understanding the mystery of gratitude.

In Luke 7: 36–47, a woman, described as a "sinner," learnt that Jesus was dining at a Pharisee's house and rushed there, uninvited. Breaching the protocols of society and ignoring the taunts of men, she wept at His feet, cleaned His feet with her hair and kissed them. The show of grateful worship earned her angry stares from the dignitaries at the dinner, including the host – a religious leader called Simon. Jesus, on the other hand, was moved and touched by her act of gratitude and commended her publicly (honour), forgave all her sins (redemption) and spoke words of peace to her (blessing).

The above biblical account shows that gratitude is not constrained by prevailing circumstances and expressed for human approval. Rather, it is an intimate spiritual act of worship to God carried out in truthfulness and humility as demonstrated by the woman's outpouring of love. The Lord is always touched whenever He encounters individuals with a grateful heart.

> Gratitude is one of the keys to access the ever-increasing grace of God. When gratitude becomes our lifestyle, we are able to face and surmount all of life's challenges through God's grace.

Unlike the woman who bowed down to kiss Jesus' feet, Judas Iscariot stood eye to eye with Jesus and kissed Him on the cheek. This act is symbolic of the carnal man trying to stand on the same level as God and approach God on man's terms. It is the sign of a self-reliant, unrepentant heart that does not believe it needs God's help or salvation. A self-reliant man is insubordinate to God's will and attempts to "kiss Him on the cheek" like an equal.

Judas' kiss also represents the insincere acts of gratitude we show towards one another. He kissed Jesus in anticipation of the thirty coins of silver that was to be the reward of his betrayal.

Unveiling Gratitude

Oftentimes, we also show gratitude only because of the benefits we expect to receive in return. If a reciprocal act of kindness is lacking, we become bitter. By kissing Jesus, Judas revealed Jesus to the enemies who would kill Him. Similarly, many of us give "kisses of gratitude" (false appreciation) with our lips while our hearts are filled with "daggers of death" (evil intentions and devious schemes).

God judges the motives of men, not just their actions, and this ought to make us sober and reflect on our ways. The Lord is waiting on us to practise true gratitude devoid of falsehood and pretences (Psalm 50: 23). When our heart is right with God, it flows with gratitude towards Him and overflows outwardly to those around us – in essence, gratitude becomes the lifestyle of both our inner and outer man. Gratitude is the most fertile ground for growing in virtue. What are those barriers to true gratitude?

> When gratitude is overthrown by hidden internal enemies, the practice of true gratitude becomes difficult, and these enemies can serve as the barriers to the true practice of gratitude.

Barriers to True Practice of Gratitude

Barriers are the obstacles preventing us from moving ahead to achieve a good cause. As we sojourn through life in the pursuit of purpose, we encounter several beautiful distractions that erect barriers, such as riches, ambition, self-achievement, talent and so on, to the true practice of gratitude in our lives. They are beautiful distractions because they subtly draw us apart or separate us from God's will – to be thankful and obedient to God's will. Satan was a beautiful distraction to Eve, which separated her from God's will.[14] Beautiful distractions never appear as distractions at the beginning until the damage is done. Likewise, we sometimes find ourselves wrestling with internal enemies, such as avariciousness, envy, anger, selfishness, among others, that become critical barriers to the true practice of gratitude. Unless these internal enemies are not destroyed, being thankful will be difficult, so does fulfilling God's will. These hidden enemies serve as the incubators of ingratitude.

The lack of gratitude can make us encounter negative emotions that may become the barriers to living a life of gratitude as instructed by God. These barriers need to be overcome so that unadulterated gratitude can be expressed. The barriers to gratitude are things that please the carnal (outward) man, natural proclivities of man unredeemed by Jesus Christ. In the following sections, I briefly discuss three principal barriers that are the basis for all other distractions or barriers to gratitude: *covetousness, murmuring and pride.*

What are these barriers, their implications and their remedies?

Covetousness
Overview of Covetousness

The Greek term for covetousness, or greed, is "pleonexia," which comes from two roots: "pleon," which means *more*, and "echo," which means *to have* or *to possess*. Pleonexia, therefore, means a desire to have more than we already have.

> *Watch out! Be on your guard against all kinds of greed; a man's life does not consist in the abundance of his possessions. (Luke 12:15)*

The above verse implies that the pursuit of power, position and possessions are perilous poisons that can distract the heart of man from being grateful for what they have or had been given by God. Humanly seeking these can lead to many temptations, which chain our affections to the things of the world rather than seeking the things above.[15] Simply put, covetousness is a spirit or an attitude of discontentment with our possessions, position, person, place or circumstances. Covetousness is the absence of a heart of thanksgiving and gratitude.

> The profanity of covetousness is that it destroys gratitude by substituting greed for character.

Sin of Covetousness and Its Consequences

Covetousness is the strong desire to have that which belongs to another. Coveting anything that belongs to our neighbours, including their house, wife, servants, ox or donkey, among others, is a grievous offense according to the Scripture, as the tenth commandment forbids it.[16] The sin of covetousness is not discussed much these days, as it has become a respectable sin, a sin that is tolerated, even in the Church and among ministers. The primary reason for such a change in attitude is that we are so deceived by this sin that we no longer see it as a sin but regard it as an ambition and a wheel to propel the fulfilling of destiny. More so, this sin is well tolerated because gratitude and thanksgiving, which are the will of God for us,[17] have been neglected because of man's own agenda.

Covetousness, as a respectable sin, is a spiritual and moral malignancy. When left unimpeded, covetousness spreads throughout our inner mind and contaminates or destroys the potency of gratitude.[18] Covetousness is the sin of desiring what God has not given us, a state of being in disagreement with God concerning what He has willed for us. Living in this state makes it difficult to express gratitude. Often, the covetous imprudently believe that their lives will be happier and more enjoyable if they have all they desire. Being covetous indirectly indoctrinates us to think that we know better than God regarding what we need to have a good life on this earth, which becomes a barrier to really appreciate what God has willed and planed for us.

The Scriptures expose that at the bottom of covetousness is idolatry. For instance, Ephesians 5:5 explains that a *"covetous man...is an idolater."* This implies that covetousness is the sin of setting one's heart on something other than God. The object of coveting controls the covetous and makes them solely focus on their desires and pursuits in life more than anything else, making them neglect the will and love of God for them. Covetousness is an act of having something other than God at the centre of our heart and life. To be of gratitude, God must be at the centre of our heart and life, which is the first and great commandment taught by Jesus.[19]

Covetousness is a state where the greed in our heart paralyses our spirit from appreciating God and others (Exodus 20: 17). It is a perpetual dissatisfaction with one's self caused by a longing for the things of others. The biblical expression "give thanks" or thanksgiving speaks of two actions: giving and thanking. These two actions are antithetical to covetousness. Covetousness is the opposite of contentment. The absence of contentment (gratitude and humility) is the birth of covetousness in the heart. Covetousness comes from a heart that is selfishly motivated instead of being spiritually motivated (Mark 7: 21).

Covetousness has been called "the mother of sin" because the desire to sin first begins in the heart before it expresses itself in action. Covetousness may not appear as bad as other more outward sins. However, in fact, it is one of the worst sins because it spawns so many others. For example, covetousness fosters envy, worry and hatred. Jesus warned about covetousness as follows:

> *Take heed, and beware of covetousness: for a man's life consisteth not in the abundance of the things which he possesseth. (Luke 12:15)*

God also spoke about the sin of covetousness in the Book of Exodus:

> *THOU SHALT NOT COVET thy neighbour's house, THOU SHALT NOT COVET thy neighbour's wife, nor his manservant, nor his maidservant, nor his ox, nor his ass, nor any thing that is thy neighbour's. (Exodus 20:17)*

Unveiling Gratitude

The depths of covetousness as seen in the above text reaches beneath the external aspects of our conduct to the hidden thoughts of the inner man (the mind, the heart and the will) and condemns sin when it is first entertained in the affections.[20] In other words, covetousness is the worship of the self, which is the embodiment of all evil. When the self sits upon the throne of the heart, we become servants to everything of this life to gain gratification from fleshy and selfish desires. Selfishness is essentially a declaration of "my right to my own self to get whatever I want for my pleasure and for my glory without minding who is hurt or affected in the process of achieving my glory." This is a heart that is in rebellion against God, and if this spirit is not broken, it will be impossible to unveil gratitude and lead a life God expects us to live. Covetousness has deadly consequences that may not be imprinted on the heart at the time of action.

> The curse of covetousness is that it deceives you, destroys your destiny by your own hands, taking you out of grace to be disgraced.

Covetousness has the power to deceive, dominate and destroy us. For example, Achan's covetousness led to disobedience (theft) and ultimately his death and that of his family (Joshua 7). David's covetousness led to adultery and murder (2 Samuel 11). Ahab's covetousness led to the murder of Naboth (1 King 21: 1–16). Ananias and Sapphira's covetousness made them lie to the Holy Spirit, which ultimately resulted in their death (Acts 5). Covetousness has a deceiving power,[21] and we can be easily misled by it without recognising that we are committing the sin. Those who covet strongly desire the belongings of others and lack gratitude for what they have been given. Covetousness destroys the ability to be grateful, as gratitude comes from a pure and honest heart, ever rejoicing in what it has.

Covetousness has a subtle way of pushing the heart of gratitude aside to blind the soul into believing a lie that we (believers) have the right to do with ourselves as we please, and we say to God,

"You have given me power to do all things." Coveting is never the result of not having something, but it arises because we refuse to be appreciative and grateful for what we have and are unable to believe we really have the best thing to be what God has made us to be.

Gratitude Overpowers Covetousness

Gratitude arises from a contemplation of the goodness of God and not the many things we desire to have. A covetous heart can be avoided by having a heart of gratitude. Thus, gratitude is the remedy for covetousness, as Christ Jesus *"according to his divine power hath given unto us all things that pertain unto life and godliness, through the knowledge of him that hath called us to glory and virtue."*[22] When we are solely focused on wants and perceived needs, seeing the abundance God has already granted in our lives becomes difficult. Therefore, focus on what God has given us to bring forth greater blessings by being grateful. Gratitude destroys and disarms covetousness and its power, making you a victor where you once thought that you were a loser or failure.

Gratitude empowers you to see God working in your future, thereby breaking not just the barriers of gratitude but also limitations. Often times, thankful and grateful people have neither the time nor the disposition to be covetous or murmur, as they are busy securing the great things they see in their future through the lens of gratitude.

> The ungrateful heart is endlessly murmuring about dissatisfaction, and it is by listening to these murmurs that one hears the Devil's lies and falls out of place.

A covetous spirit is a fertile breeding ground for murmuring and a deadly barrier to the practice of gratitude. Make no mistake, murmuring is a terrible sin and can imprison you in directionless wilderness. Murmuring aggravates the lack of satisfaction and can possible keep one unhappy and perhaps offend God.

What is the barrier of murmuring, and how can it affect unveiling gratitude?

Murmuring

Overview of Murmuring

Murmuring is also known as complaining or grumbling. In this book, I describe murmuring as the second principal barrier to gratitude.[23] Murmuring can be interchanged with complaining or grumbling, and these three terms can be used at the same time if the need for such arises to emphasise an expression. Murmuring is the repeated voicing of one's discontentment or dissatisfaction over the situation *God has placed one in*. Apart from discontentment or dissatisfaction, murmuring can come from several other sources such as self-pity, the desire for sympathy, anger, bitterness and unbelief.

Sin of Murmuring and Its Consequences

Murmuring is a vile impiety, a great sin that destroys the heart from being appreciative. At the core, it is a sin of discontentment, characterised by a lack of faith in God. Although many of us murmur/complain to gain human sympathy, it only attracts God's anger and keeps us stuck at the same spot (Exodus 16: 9–12). We cannot murmur and express gratitude at the same time.

Whenever we choose to be grateful, we disarm the power of discontentment, which is the source of murmuring. While gratitude is born out of contentment through the Spirit of God that speaks of much grace, strength and beauty, murmuring speaks of corruption, strong rebellion and the vile dishonesty of the heart.

> The Devil is the most discontented, proudest and dejected creature; being of discontent is living the

> Devil's lifestyle, as gratitude is never part of his character.

The Lucifer was the first grumbler/murmurer, and the onset of his fall from heaven was a result of his dissatisfaction with his position and the desire and ambition to be like God.[24]

> *And all the children of Israel murmured against Moses and against Aaron: and the whole congregation said unto them, Would God that we had died in the land of Egypt! or would God we had died in this wilderness... (Numbers 14: 1–3)*

The Israelites murmured against their gracious and loving God, and their murmurings displeased God because He expected a heart of gratitude from them.

Some would argue that the Israelites were murmuring against Moses and not intentionally murmuring against God, especially in Exodus 16.[25] However, regardless of whether to Moses or God, murmuring is a sin and cannot create a heart of gratitude and enable us to live in thankfulness, which are God's will for us.[26] Sadly, in this present world of covetousness, many of us[27] are murmurers, complainers and grumblers because we are not satisfied with the grace and love God has given us.

Unthankfulness or ingratitude is the act of not showing appreciation for the things received or given by God through grace. As grace has been given to us freely, we must be grateful at all times, not only when we abound in material wealth but also when tormented and tested like Job.[28] We must always be appreciative of God's goodness regardless of the form in which it comes.[29]

> The genesis of murmuring is the exodus of gratitude, leaving pessimistic spirit to drag us into the strong room of doubt and disobedience.

Regarding the goodness of God, murmuring implies a contempt of and ingratitude towards the goodness of God. When we repine and murmur, it shows a contempt of God's goodness to us and the failure to express thanks to God for His many blessings we don't deserve. Despising God's goodness is a sin, as it provokes God. We develop spiritual amnesia when we forget God's goodness and benefits like the Israelites did after God's gracious and miraculous deliverance of them out of Egypt. The Israelites, even after experiencing God's incredible and incomprehensible miracles and plundering Egyptian wealth, still complained bitterly about the unattractive accommodation God provided them in the desert.

A contextual examination of the Israelites' behaviour reveals that their complaining was more of unfaithfulness, discontentment and ingratitude than that of just physical discomfort. Unfaithfulness blocks our spiritual understanding about God's benevolence, rendering it difficult to truly express gratitude and give thanks in all situations, which the Scriptures say we should do.[30] As believers, we should engage in not only relentless prayer but also unceasing and abounding thanksgiving. Put simply, believers' prayers should be rooted in thanksgiving. As possessing a thankful spirit is the will and desire of God, it should be encouraged. God by giving us His only begotten Son as the gift of life has automatically placed believers under the obligation of lasting thanksgiving, not as an option but a necessity.

Murmuring is not the heart's response to circumstances but to God. When we murmur, grumble or complain about our circumstances, we are not murmuring against the situation or people we're amidst but against God. Murmuring will most likely make us envious of others[31] and impatient,[32] prompting us to take things into our own hands,[33] preventing us from listening to God voice and believing His word.[34]

This resonates with Paul's instruction to the believers at Philippi that they should do all things without murmuring or complaining so that they may become blameless and harmless amidst the perverse generation.[35]

The dissatisfaction of our satisfaction and the discontentment of our contentment are dissentient to God's divine providence and decree and are disputants to gratitude and defilers of thanksgiving.

Murmuring cuts off our vision for the future. When our eyes are set on the Promised Land, murmuring becomes a taboo. Oftentimes, we end up stuck in our wilderness because we hurt God with our murmuring rather than pleasing Him with our heart of faith, trust and obedience (humility and meekness). Murmuring, complaining and whining concur with Satan in that there is no hope for our future. Gratitude empowers us to see the light and exceeding greatness in our future. Murmuring only invites greater adversity, such as punishment, sickness, captivity, and activates the sleeping curse.[36] Consequently, the cure for murmuring is wearing the garment of praise, which is expressed in gratitude, gratefulness and thanksgiving.

Gratitude Overpowers Murmuring

A heart of gratitude empowers us to live without murmuring and complaining in our homes, offices, businesses, relationships and ministries. The spirit of gratitude enables us to understand and appreciate other people's weakness and faults and be prepared to bear with them[37] and make people better, rather than murmuring and complaining about them, which lead to hurt, bitterness or gossip and, ultimately, gross sin.

To dismantle and destroy the barrier of murmuring to live a life of gratitude as instructed by God,[38] we must love each other, as love covers a multitude of sins, in which murmuring is included.[39] Murmuring is not only complaining about a situation[40] and grumbling over the seemly offenses and shortcoming of others[41] but also having a critical and judgemental spirit that always judges others.[42] We should be watchful and prayerful not to judge others by their actions via the intentions of our heart, as this affects our unveiling of gratitude through hospitality.

> 1 Peter 4: 9 emphasises God's intention for us to be hospitable to one another without complaints. Murmuring should not be part of our Christian life. To please God for His benefits we receive daily, we must run away from murmuring.

In conclusion, summarising from a cardiovascular medicine perspective, if you have a spirit of murmuring, you are suffering from a "chronic heart murmuring disease." This means there are other serious risk factors associated with your heart murmuring disease. Your heart murmuring disease suggests that you likely have a discontent (congenital) heart problem, displeasure (valve) heart problem and dissatisfaction (endocarditis) heart problem. All these risk factors (heart problems) prevent the heart from pumping and circulating enough blood required by the body, which may result in you getting exhausted so quickly that you cannot function properly because you are not breathing well (not connected with God's Spirit). At this time, you begin to suffer from envy (chest pain), quarrelling (hypertension) and depression (heart failure), and if no preventative measures are undertaken to curb this, your heart could shut down and your destiny terminated. Remember, the act of murmuring is not so much the problem but how it leaves our heart drained and damaged.

Thus, the spiritual therapy for murmuring is *gratitude*. Gratitude and thanksgiving forever stand in full opposition to all murmurings against God's dealings with us. When we refuse to deal with the spirit of murmuring, pride is born, a bigger sin, which leads us to the third barrier to gratitude – *pride*. Pride is also a spiritual circulatory heart disease that affects and destroys our spiritual sensitivity by producing the toxin ingratitude. What is the barrier of pride?

Pride

Overview of Pride

Pride is the third barrier to gratitude. Pride can have a wide variety of meanings. It can be anything from narcissism to self-confidence to self-respect. However, the meaning, nature or concept of pride here are viewed from the spectrum and lens of the Scriptures.

Like the other barriers to gratitude, pride is also a terrible and deadly sin. Pride turned an angel into the Devil. Pride is primarily worshipping the self over God. In other words, pride is the excessive belief in one's abilities that hampers one's acknowledgment or acceptance of God's grace. It is a bid to be self-reliant outside of God, which agrees with Baruch Spinoza's reflection that "pride is thinking more highly of oneself than is just, out of love for oneself."[43]

Many of us associate pride with acts of arrogance and condescension; while these are all different forms of pride, another variant of pride is *self-righteousness* – a belief that we are somehow morally superior to others and merit God's blessings for our righteous acts. This form of pride is equally deadly. God through His Word has warned us to guard our hearts against pride lest we too *"fall into the same condemnation as the Devil."* To guard our heart, apart from renewing our mind daily[44] through the Word of God by studying, meditating,[45] praying and fasting,[46] we should be grateful and thankful, which involve the acts of humility and contentment.

> As pride is powerful enough to convert an angel to a devil, so is humility powerful to make man angelic, as it empowers and energises to do great works of benevolence.

Apostle Paul advises us to have Christ's attitude. Although Christ was in the form of God, He did not regard Himself equal to

God but emptied Himself, took human likeness and humbled Himself according to His Father's will, obedient to death on the Cross. Therefore, God greatly exalted Him and bestowed upon Him the name above every name.[47] Christ didn't allow pride to overshadow Him, and He was filled with gratitude to be called names that were not His so that we could be saved. If the Lord Himself was humble, who are we then to stand firm in pride and arrogance?

As much as pride is a dangerous spiritual disease, diagnosing it can be difficult and challenging at times for some. Pride affects our eyesight, making us see ourselves through a lens that taints and distorts reality. Pride paints our ugliness in sin as beautiful and commendable and makes us see gratitude as weakness and cowardice.

Sin of Pride and Its Consequences

Pride revolts against God's authority, God's law and God's rule, and for this reason, thankfulness and appreciation are never expressed, as appreciating authorities, rules, things or people we condemn is challenging. God detests pride. He even hates a proud look.[48] God's repugnance of pride is unalterable, for *"everyone that is proud in heart is an abomination to the Lord."*[49] At creation, God did not make the Devil; Lucifer became the Devil when he arrogantly became infatuated with himself.[50] It is imperative we know that self-will displaces God's will and prompts the Devil to emerge. Pride destroys, demotes and disgraces us openly. We should not take glory in the flesh but in the grace that has been granted to us, as only when we are being appreciative can pride be destroyed.

The Bible explicitly states that we have all fallen short of God's glory, that we do not merit His blessings and that we are who we are only by the grace of God. In a nutshell, the gospel of redemption is that man did not/could not reach God; God (in the person of Jesus Christ) reached man, which Paul explains as follows:

> *For all have sinned, and come short of the glory of God; Being justified freely by his grace through the redemption that is in Christ Jesus. (Romans 3: 23–24)*

The above realisation should impact the way we relate to others. When we know we are undeserving recipients of God's grace, we will no longer be quick to judge or condemn others; there will be no room in our hearts for pride but only gratitude to the God of all grace.

The sin of pride not only prompts us to be a fault-finder, filtering out the negatives we see in ourselves, but also makes us find faults with God's goodness in others. Pride specialises in sifting others, digging out only their faults but never their positive attributes. When pride becomes our strength, we take full credit for our achievements without expressing gratitude to God or others. While boasting seeks adulation, pride judges the weaknesses of others by disapproving or belittling them publicly in an interior manner. The recognition of grace humbles us and prevents us from being a fault-finder.[51]

The sin of pride transformed Lucifer, an anointed cherub of God, the very "seal of perfection, full of wisdom and perfect in beauty,"[52] into Satan, the Devil, the father of lies, the one for whom Hell itself was created.[53] The sin of pride is characterised by the philosophy "Me, I and Myself" (MIM). The words "pride" and "sin" have "I" at the centre.[54] One of the reasons behind splintered relationships, broken marriages and church splits is pride, as pride stirs up contention.[55]

A slanderer is a fool[56] and lacks a heart of gratitude and humility to see grace at work in the lives of others. Pride also gives birth to deadly gossip, evil speaking and slander, which are the direct results of pride. A heart that expresses gratitude does not engage in gossip. A heart of gratitude is having the nature of God and not necessarily being blessed with materials things or achievements.[57] The word "devil" comes from the word *diabolos*, which means slanderer.

> He who listens to gossips carries the Devil in his ears, and he who spreads gossips speaks on behalf of the Devil, as the Devil only hired him as a critic to cause contention.

The proud delude themselves, causing conflicts and tension wherever they go because they never understand the evil in their heart. However, the thankful, the grateful and those who unveil gratitude appreciate the grace of God and understand the imperfections of others because they acknowledge through gratitude that they are imperfect as well.[58] Pride in our illusory qualities leads to personal bondage, social hatred and unthankfulness.

Gratitude Overpowers Pride

We can, therefore, conclude that gratitude goes beyond maintaining a positive psychological state or releasing some sort of "spiritual cause-and-effect force of karma." Understanding gratitude from God's perspective brings us into deeper communion with God and fills us with grace towards men. When gratitude becomes our lifestyle, we grow in the grace of God and our lives manifest His glory in ever-increasing measure. The unveiling of the mystery of gratitude comes with the understanding of gratitude, especially from God's perspective. Having a clear understanding of godly gratitude empowers us to really live the life God expects from us, as noted in 1 Thessalonians 5: 18.[59]

Apart from gratitude being a mystery to those whom it's yet to be unveiled, gratitude is also a doctrine that needs to be taught. Jesus taught His disciples in the Sermon on the Mount that *"blessed are the meek: for they shall inherit the earth."*[60] Gratitude, therefore, must be taught and encouraged, as it is the *will* of God for us.

The unveiling of gratitude progresses through the sanctification and brokenness of the inner man[61] and is never completed until we are glorified, as we are indebted[62] to Christ who has given us every good thing pertaining to life and eternal life.[63] We are all debtors to God's infinite grace, a debt we can never repay.[64] This must be taught and understood to unveil the mystery and attitude of gratitude to live in God's *will* as instructed in 1 Thessalonians 5:18. The significance of the doctrine and attitude of gratitude is in the "teaching" that all may come to the understanding of gratitude's spiritual implication and essence. Paul encouraged Titus that *"for we ourselves also were sometimes foolish, disobedient, deceived, serving divers lusts and pleasures, living in malice and envy, hateful, and hating one another"* (Titus 3:3).

As believers, we are indebted to teach and practise gratitude, as it is profitable unto all men. Consequently, when gratitude is taught, learnt and practised, it has positive effects on our moods, relationships, and learning. Being grateful to a benefactor opens up a more relational dimension, where the benefactor is acknowledged, thereby creating a lasting relationship-binding love. If gratitude is to be taught, is gratitude then a doctrine? What then are the doctrine and attitude of gratitude?

Endnotes

1 Charles H. Spurgeon, Commentary on Matthew: The Gospel of the Kingdom (The Banner of Truth Trust, UK, 2010), pp. 92–104. Also see R. C. H. Lenski, The Interpretation of Matthew's Gospel (Minneapolis, 1943) p. 528.

2 Romans 9: 23–24

3 Romans 9: 23–24

4 Mark 4: 11 – "And He said to them, 'To you it has been given to know the mystery of the kingdom of God; but to those who are outside, all things come in parables'." In Matthew 13, Jesus presented through the seven parables the mysteries of the Kingdom. Only Matthew has recorded the seven parables. Matthew 13 speaks mostly about the period of the Kingdom in its mystery form. Without a clear understanding of these mysteries of the Kingdom, we may not fully respond to God's grace and reveal His glory in the form of gratitude for the world to see Him.

5 1 Timothy 3: 9 – "Holding the mystery of the faith with a pure conscience." The faith that Paul is speaking of here is a special kind of faith, a faith rooted in Christ, for He is the truth and He is infallible. Faith not rooted in truth will not bring us the desired results; likewise, gratitude not rooted in truth will not bring out godliness.

6 Thomas A. Kempis, The Imitation of Christ (London; UK, Penguin Classics; New Impression edition) p. 82.

7 1 Thessalonians 5: 18

8 A. M., Wood, Froh, J. J., & Geraghty, A. A. Gratitude and well-being: A review and theoretical integration. Clinical Psychology Review, (2010. 30(7), pp. 890–905).

9 Robert A. Emmons and Michael E. McCullough, The Psychology of Gratitude (Oxford University Press, USA, 2004) p. 5.

10 Jens Uhder, "The Benefits of Gratitude in Spiritual Formation: Collaborative of Gratefulness in a Christian Church Community" (2016. Doctor of Psychology (PsyD) Paper 193. p. 2).

11 C. Peterson, & M.E. Seligman, Character, Strengths and Virtues: A Classification and Handbook. (New York: Oxford University Press/Washington, DC: American Psychological Association, 2004).

12 Robert A. Emmons, Gratitude Works: A 21-Day Program for Creating Emotional Prosperity (San Francisco; CA, Jossey Bass, 2013), pp. 75–104.

13 Gratefulness here means to count our blessings and to be mindful of all the benefits we receive from God, knowingly and unknowingly. See Psalm 68: 19, Psalm 103: 2, Ephesians 5: 20, 1 Thessalonians 5: 16–18

14 Genesis 1–3

15 Colossians 3: 1–3 – "1 If ye then be risen with Christ, seek those things which are above, where Christ sitteth on the right hand of God. 2 Set your affection on things above, not on things on the earth. 3. For ye are dead, and your life is hid with Christ in God."

16 Exodus 20: 17

17 1 Thessalonians 5: 18 – "In everything give thanks: for this is the will of God in Christ Jesus concerning you."

18 Ephesians 5: 1–5 – Covetousness is the root of all kinds of sins that Jesus warned about. See Luke 12: 15

19 Matthew 22: 37–38 – "37. Jesus said unto him, 'Thou shalt love the Lord thy God with all thy heart, and with all thy soul, and with all thy mind. 38. This is the first and great commandment'."

20 James 1: 14–15 – "But every man is tempted, when he is drawn away of his own lust, and enticed. Then when lust hath conceived, it bringeth forth sin: and sin, when it is finished, bringeth forth death." Likewise, Mark 7: 21–23 explains that everyone by nature possesses this evil heart of covetousness, for out of the heart of man emanates all sin. Till the inner man is broken to be of God's nature, pure gratitude cannot be expressed in its godly form.

21 Covetousness is very deceitful.

22 2 Peter 1: 3

23 In this book, I discuss only three principal barriers to gratitude, as there are many more barriers to divine gratitude.

24 Isaiah 14: 12–17. See Isaiah 14: 14 – "I will ascend above the heights of the clouds; I will be like the most High."

25 See Dean S. McBride, "Transcendent Authority: The Role of Moses in Old Testament Traditions," Int44 (July 1990): 233. Also see M. M. Kalisch, Exodus (London: Longman, Brown, Green and Longmans, 1855), p. 285.

26 1 Thessalonians 5: 18 – "In everything give thanks: for this is the will of God in Christ Jesus concerning you."

27 Us here refers to believers.

28 Job.1: 20 – "Then Job arose, and rent his mantle, and shaved his head, and fell down upon the ground, and worshipped. In his calamity, he worshipped the Lord – he was filled with the spirit of gratefulness that he didn't sin either through murmuring or anger."

29 Ephesians 5: 20

30 1 Thessalonians 5: 18

31 Numbers 16

32 Exodus 32

33 Numbers 16, Exodus 32

34 Numbers 14, 20

35 Philippians 2: 14–16 – "14 Do all things without murmurings and disputings: 15 That ye may be blameless and harmless, the sons of God, without rebuke, in the midst of a crooked and perverse nation, among whom ye shine as lights in the world; 16 Holding forth the word of life; that I may rejoice in the day of Christ, that I have not run in vain, neither laboured in vain."

36 Numbers 14: 27–29

37 James 5: 9 – "Grudge not one against another, brethren, lest ye be condemned: behold, the judge standeth before the door." Colossians 3: 13 – "Forbearing one another, and forgiving one another, if any man have a quarrel against any: even as Christ forgave you, so also do ye."

38 1 Thessalonians 5: 18 – "In everything give thanks: for this is the will of God in Christ Jesus concerning you."

39 1 Peter 4: 8–10 – "8 And above all things have fervent charity among yourselves: for charity shall cover the multitude of sins. 9 Use hospitality one to another without grudging. 10 As every man hath received the gift, even so minister the same one to another, as good stewards of the manifold grace of God."

40 Numbers 14: 1–3

41 Exodus 16

42 Romans 14: 10–13: A "critical spirit" is an obsessive attitude of criticism and fault-finding, which seeks to tear down others rather than build them up. It is destructive criticism. A critical spirit dwells on the negative and looks for flaws rather than positive qualities in others.

43 J. Neu, "Pride and identity." In R. C. Solomon (Ed.), Wicked Pleasures: Meditations on the Seven "Deadly" Sins (Lanham: Rowman & Littlefield, 1999), pp. 51–79.

44 Romans 12: 1–2

45 Joshua 1: 6-9

46 Philippians 4: 3

47 Philippians 2: 4–11

48 Proverb 6: 16–17

49 Proverb 16: 5

50 Isaiah 14: 12–14

51 Gratitude is unveiled when we appreciate others, regardless of their state, and even see them better than us even with their so-called faults, as we all are products of grace, working at different speed levels.

52 Ezekiel 28: 12

53 John 8: 44, Matthew 25: 41

54 Lucifer said in his heart, "I will ascend into heaven, I will exalt my throne above the stars of God; I will also sit on the mount of

the congregation on the farthest sides of the north; I will ascend above the heights of the clouds, I will be like the Most High."

55 Proverbs 13: 10

56 Proverb. 10: 18, see Psalm 14

57 "Materials things or achievements" are important, and we should be grateful to God for the grace to achieve them, but they should not be the only basis to express gratitude. Gratitude should be expressed in every situation – the comprehensible and the incomprehensible. Job experienced both comprehensible situations (When all was well, he understood God's goodness and was grateful and thankful) and incomprehensible situations (When in his calamity, he didn't understand anything that was happening. Yet in it all, he was grateful and thankful), for which God rewarded him duly – Job 1.

58 Romans 14: 4

59 1 Thessalonians 5: 18 – "In everything give thanks; for this is the will of God in Christ Jesus for you."

60 Matthew 5: 5

61 Romans 12: 1–2

62 The realisation of our powerlessness without the divine help of God makes us to fully rely on God's grace as our true source of strength to overcome and be grateful at all times.

63 2 Peter 1: 3 – "According as his divine power hath given unto us all things that pertain unto life and godliness, through the knowledge of him that hath called us to glory and virtue."

64 Romans 8: 12–14

Chapter Four

Doctrine and Attitude of Gratitude

In this chapter, I aim to bring to the fore the essence of biblical gratitude as a Christian doctrine, as doing so is timely, meaningful and relevant at this juncture. Thankfulness resonates with the heartbeat of God, and our heartfelt gratitude to the almighty God, expressed in unfeigned response to His love, righteousness and mercy, places us before Him in honour and spiritual integrity. The key spiritual elements of our acts of Christian gratitude – humility, adoration, adulation, worship – constitute a true reciprocal response of the our (believers') love for God's many gracious benefits bestowed on us all as humanity, which are too many to count, too many to list.

Biblical doctrines seek to describe the way things are in the eyes and mind of our sublime God. It points us to the truth of Christ's gospel so that we may approach thereto and graciously act upon that truth accordingly. The overall eternal design of God is that we all be established in the firm foundation and true knowledge of Christ, which is born out of godly obedience. Gratitude is the culmination of our worship. It is in this context that I have attributed the status of "doctrine" to the Christian attitude of gratitude.

A doctrine is not merely a wishful idea, perfunctory religious reflection or figment of human imagination. It is a reality of human mental reaction and response to the historical actions of God. In this regard, Alistair E. McGrath asserts as follows:

> *Doctrine makes truth-claims. To speak of doctrine as "truth" is rightly to draw attention to the fundamental Christian conviction that doctrine claims to make significant and justifiable statements about the order*

> *of things, about the way things are. Nevertheless, it is also concerned with maintaining the possibility of encountering the truth, which the Christian tradition firmly locates in Jesus Christ as the source of her identity.*[1]

McGrath states further that a biblical doctrine describes what Christians believe to be true and also invites those outside the Christian church to believe in this truth. I can safely relate and apply this truism to other religions or the secular world, for instance, in which the doctrine of gratitude is an especially acknowledged spiritual virtue. I am not saying here that the core doctrinal beliefs of the Christian faith and practices are "on all fours" with that of other religions. In fact, it is far from it! What I am driving at is that the attitude of gratitude is significantly relational and that its spiritual values span across the philosophical principles of many religions and social institutions.

Gratitude is the right attitude and is inspired by God. It is concerning this point that my deepest interest is tickled. The Bible represents a guiding spiritual norm on the subject of gratitude and perhaps very many other religious books of instruction. This means that the act of gratitude is a key priority in the human worship of God, which also manifests in our relationships with others. It is, therefore, a cardinal doctrine of faith, and the doctrine of gratitude to God is sacrosanct. God commands it; God demands it; God rewards it. The Christian practice of gratitude, therefore, is richly rewarding.

The expression of gratitude is beyond religion. It is an innate spiritual response and responsibility of us as believers to be thankful to the Lord for all the benefits bestowed upon us all. We as Christians owe to God a moral and spiritual duty to be grateful beyond measure and in all things, particularly for the redemption of humanity. In this, we have reason to rejoice in the love, grace, forgiveness and reconciliation procured on the Cross. We rejoice in God Himself and are immensely grateful to Him for giving His only begotten Son to be shamefully crucified on the Cross. It was a deliberate act on the part of God and consistent with the divine plan of ages to allow Christ to die on the Cross for a lost world. It is the will of God as the Bible states:

> *Yet it pleased the Lord to bruise him; he hath put him to grief: when thou shalt make his soul an offering for sin, he shall see his seed, he shall prolong his days, and the pleasure of the Lord shall prosper in his hand. (Isaiah 53:10)²*

Our gratitude is our response to the will of God, but the will of God expresses more than a mere doctrine. It intersects with our lives as Christians on a daily basis. The doctrine of gratitude is concerned with expressing and defending the trustworthiness of God. It also explains and defends His integrity, truthfulness and justice. God demonstrated His mercy and justice on the Cross. Calvary has become our symbolic reference to gratitude, where the Passover Lamb was slain, the Sin offering was made and the suffering Servant was crucified. Calvary was not a mere historical episode; it was a grand design of God in accordance with His pre-determinate counsel:

> *For Christ also hath once suffered for sins, the just for the unjust, that he might bring us to God...(1 Peter 3:18)*

This was a once-and-for-all sacrifice through which the sufferings of Christ brought us back to God. Christ was ultimately delivered up by the *"determinate counsel and foreknowledge of God"* (Acts 2: 23). If we can trust God enough for the salvation of our souls, then we must be grateful for the offer of Christ's sacrifice on the Cross of Calvary.

In conclusion, gratitude is basic Christian ethics. Gratitude is the honest response of a beneficiary to the beneficence of a benefactor. The doctrine of gratitude explains that gratitude born from a heart of thankfulness or gratefulness is a form of worship, and the

Church Age worshippers acknowledged and practised gratitude[3] and received rewards related to God's grace.

> The breadth of circumstances in which we invoke gratitude terms would suggest that gratitude, generally, is the response a person should have to something good – that is, to benefit or "favour."[4]

Gratitude, a quintessence of thanksgiving, gratefulness and appreciation, is a part of our spiritual life and worship.[5] Gratitude being a doctrine means it is not some superficial, ephemeral response towards some beneficence received but the act of an incessant mental attitude produced by the Holy Spirit, as we are genuinely equipped, taught and rooted in the Word of God.[6]

We are to convey gratitude through our attitude for encouraging others to lead a Christ-centred life and be hopeful. Appreciating other brethren increases their faith, empowers them to be steadfast and strengthens their love for one another to wax stronger. Apostle Paul encouraged us to be bound by thanks, appreciating each other, in prayers, words or deeds.[7] By doing this, the attitude of gratitude is unveiled

An attitude of gratitude is born of the Spirit and a part of God's will for us. Possessing an attitude of gratitude is not "thanking" God because we want to impress Him or make Him feel good about us or an obligation to meet some spiritual requirement to receive something from Him. What is then an attitude of gratitude?

Attitude of Gratitude

In a general sense, an attitude is a human behavioural response to the environment one is in, motivated by thinking and/or feeling about something or someone. This description is a psychological construct usually associated with a person's personality and dispositions to life. Human attitudes and behaviour are, therefore, intricately intertwined. In this book, however, I aim to explore the meaning and virtue of *attitude* within the context of Christian spirituality.

The following is the take of Selwyn Hughes on Christian attitudes:

> Our attitudes have a tremendous and powerful influence upon every part of our being-physical as well as emotional. Man is a unit made up of spirit, soul and body, and he cannot be sick in one part without passing on the sickness to other parts. The attitudes we hold in our minds do not stay merely as attitudes- they pass over into definite physical effects. God has so designed our beings that the right attitudes produce the right effects in our bodies.[8]

The Bible is replete with passages that describe the attitudes of God. The attitudes of God indicate the ways in which He relates to His people, which suggests what the corresponding behaviour and attitudes of Christian believers should be towards Him. There is a famous maxim that "to whom much is given much is expected."[9] The attributes of God are His attitudes. Our attitudes as Christians must show that we are the children of God. God's attributes of love, compassion, grace, mercy, patience and faithfulness must be humbly reciprocated by our attitudes of gratitude, trust, faith, love, hope, holiness, prayerfulness, self-denial, praise and reverence. We must eschew all forms of ingratitude and rebellion against God. We must adopt and live a truly sanctified life. God wants us to be thankful, and we must embrace and practise this aspiration with the whole of our being. No shortcut exists to walking with God outside of obedience and gratitude.

Hence, Apostle Paul in Romans 12: 1–2, encouraged us to be a "living sacrifice." For us to be a living sacrifice, the sense of gratitude should be activated, as we cannot love God without appreciating who He is. In other words, being a living sacrifice to God in gratitude is the least we can give to God in acknowledgement of and gratitude for His benevolence – gracious mercy. I, therefore, wish to express here that gratitude is far beyond words of pleasantry but divine in nature, an acknowledgement of absolute dependence on God. In furtherance to this, our lived life after we are redeemed is built on nothing less than Christ's righteousness, which becomes our righteousness through an obedient life of gratitude and implants in us the holy attitude to behold the attributes of the Holy God.

The Bible is a sacred book that gives positive direction to our lives. It tells us how to live life wisely in the will of God. It encourages reflective lives and values. It is a book of great wisdom and reflections as well as deep spiritual meditations and motivations. Yes, a book of meditations and motivation, in that when we cultivate the presence of God in meditation and prayer, our actions become motivated by the *Holy Spirit* and conformable to the will of God. Thereby, we are also motivated by wisdom and gratitude. We are grateful for what God represents in our lives and circumstances. We are grateful for having the Bible as our primary rule of faith and practice. We are not spiritually empty. We are not flying blind. We are safely navigated under the grace and watchful eyes of God. We are grateful for all His benefits. We are superlatively motivated and joyful when our heart overflows with gratitude, as God's will becomes our delight.

In view of the above, the importance or essence of being grateful (living in gratitude) as a key aspect of our Christian life cannot be overemphasised. Gratitude satisfies a moral yearning in our day-to-day interpersonal relationships as Christian believers and the true disciples of Jesus Christ. Gratitude directs our attention to who God is. It also helps us to focus and appreciate what God has graciously done for us in His sovereignty and mercy. Gratitude is our reasonable service to God and man. The whole of our being must be reverent and grateful to God.

Unveiling Gratitude

God commands an attitude of gratitude in a very significant way with a view to draw us into a special relational intimacy with Him:

> *Let us come before his presence with thanksgiving and make a joyful noise unto him with psalms. (Psalm 95: 2)*
>
> *Our gratitude is our reciprocal action of love towards God. He first loved us. We love him, because he first loved us.*
>
> *(1 John 4: 19)*
>
> *But God commendeth his love towards us, in that, while we were yet sinners, Christ died for us. (Romans 5:8)*

This is the thrust and hallmark of our gratitude. Christ died to redeem us. He saved us. Indeed, we should be grateful and always be.

The Bible aptly narrates the commandment of gratitude:

> *8 Give thanks unto the Lord, call upon his name, make known his deeds among the people. 9 Sing unto him, sing psalms unto him, talk ye of all his wondrous works. 10 Glory ye in his holy name: let the heart of them rejoice that seek the Lord. 11 Seek the Lord and his strength, seek his face continually. 12 Remember his marvellous works that he hath done, his wonders, and the judgments of his mouth. (1 Chronicles 16: 8–12)*

The above words of the Chronicler are statements of spiritual facts and indeed also a solemn call to worship and give gratitude to God. Thus, let me emphasise here that all our human life, including our entire moral life, must become worship, which stirs from a heart of gratitude. Gratitude, therefore, plays a significant role in true worship. In other words, without gratitude, worship becomes impossible, as worship is spiritual in nature and emanates from the spiritual heart of gratitude. Without worthship[10] (gratitude), there is no worship (Revelation 4:11)

The verses in Psalm 105: 1–15 are also instructively compatible with the prophetic rhythm in 1 Chronicle 16: 8–12 rendered above. The overall impression here is that God seeks our sincere gratitude and calls Israel to worship, praise, honour, obey and seek Him. Psalm 105: 1–4 particularly calls for deeper reflection and meditation. Its content encourages and promotes our attitudes of gratitude. God miraculously preserved the personal and corporate history of Israel both as a nation and a holy chosen people. The sublime virtue of gratitude is hereby inspired in the people of Israel (as indeed in us all who now live and walk in Christ), for God's great care, protection and manifold blessings. Our gratitude is, therefore, very critical to both our spiritual and physical health as well as sustenance.

Our attitude of gratitude is our testimony of God's goodness to others (Psalm 22: 22–31) and testifies of the triumph of Jesus' Cross. Christ is now the exalted redeemer and saviour whom all believers must revere and worship in spirit and truth to reveal, unveil and manifest God's Kingdom on earth – as both Christ's embassy and ambassador here on earth.[11] To unveil divine gratitude and fulfil God's command,[12] we must be reconciled in God's will.

In conclusion, gratitude is a key spiritual discipline for the Christian life. Gratitude is an attitude. Our attitude is a choice. We must develop the attitude of gratitude. It is a crucial law of life and success. It enhances our spiritual and physical health. We cannot claim that our lives are so beset with pains, troubles and trials that we really have nothing for which to be grateful. But if we cultivate a reflective life and embrace the right perspective, we surely will find that there is something to be grateful for in every situation of our lives.

Unveiling Gratitude

An attitude of gratitude unveils the companion virtues and potency of gratitude. During the most difficult and lowest moments in my life, when all familiar efforts seemed thwarted and no one seemed to understand the pain and wounds I bore, I stood grateful to God, and He was faithful, addressing my issues His own way. When we are thankful and the potency of our gratitude is at work, everything around us will begin to speak on our behalf, even when we are weak.

God taught me in the darkest room of my life that gratitude is a potent, procreant force breaking through mountainous troubled hearts to say, "It is well." Regardless of what we experience, gratitude is a companion virtue that rescues us from whatever state in which we may find ourselves. As the voice of the Lord is powerful,[13] so is gratitude powerful to calm and melt every situation, opening our eyes to the inconceivable possibilities around us.

In practising gratitude, learn to close your eyes to what you know about people and what they must have done to you and hold unto what God holds for them – love and mercy, the virtues and potency of gratitude.

> Gratitude slams shut the door of judgement on others and opens wide the door of mercy so that others can see God in you. Condemnation cannot co-exist with gratitude.

Traversing my "wilderness of life," I learnt my entire life must be of gratitude whether life itself presents us faith, hope and charity, which are fundamental for walking with God. In all situations, we must express the virtue of gratitude, as faith, hope and charity (love) are the forms of outward and social worship that need to be to be considered as we interact and relate with the environs in order to show God to others (Matthew 5: 14–16).[14]

As we live our Christian life, we should understand that there is no separation between external and social forms of worship and the reality of our personal Christian life dedicated to God, as we are to reflect and express God through our attitude at all times, concerning which Paul states as follows:

Who shall separate us from the love of Christ? Shall tribulation, or distress, or persecution, or famine, or nakedness, or peril, or sword? (Romans 8: 35–39)

In everything give thanks; for this is the will of God in Christ Jesus for you. (1 Thessalonians 5: 18)

Therefore, worship, a heart of gratitude is more related to lifestyle (virtue) rather than to liturgical performance.

Gratitude as a virtue is a gift we owe everybody in the world. As mentioned, gratitude is the overflow of a humble and meek heart expressed amongst people and to God, which makes gratitude a companion virtue. What is this companion virtue and the potency of gratitude?

Endnotes

1 Alister E. McGrath, Studies in Doctrine (Grand Rapids: Zondervan, 1997) p. 244.

2 God's redemptive plan and purpose of bringing many people to salvation through Christ have been attained. This is corroborated in Isaiah 53: 11, to the effect that the suffering of Christ the Messiah would accomplish God's divine purpose of bringing salvation to all who believe. In the process, Jesus also poured out His soul unto death.

3 Church Age worshippers acknowledged and practised the act of gratitude; thanksgiving.

4 Walker, A.D.M., 1980–1981, "Gratefulness and Gratitude," Proceedings of the Aristotelian Society, 81: pp. 39–55.

5 1 Thessalonians 5: 18

6 Colossians 2: 7 – "Rooted and built up in him, and stablished in the faith, as ye have been taught, abounding therein with thanksgiving."

7 1 Thessalonians 1: 2–3 – "2 We give thanks to God always for you all, making mention of you in our prayers. 3 Remembering without ceasing your work of faith, and labour of love, and patience of hope in our Lord Jesus Christ, in the sight of God and our Father."

8 Selwyn Hughes, The Divine Attitudes – Key Qualities for Effective Living (Great Britain, BPCC Paulton Limited, 1989) p. 6.

9 Luke 12: 48 – "But he that knew not, and did commit things worthy of stripes, shall be beaten with few stripes. For unto

whomsoever much is given, of him shall be much required: and to whom men have committed much, of him they will ask the more."

10 Only a heart of gratitude can know the *worth* of something. Without appreciating and being grateful, the worth of a thing still remains veiled. Gratitude unveils the worth of God, which produces a lifestyle of worship.

11 2 Corinthians 5: 20 – "Now then, we are ambassadors for Christ, as though God were pleading through us: we implore you on Christ's behalf, be reconciled to God."

12 1 Thessalonians 5: 18 – "In everything give thanks; for this is the will of God in Christ Jesus for you."

13 Psalm 29: 1–4 – "1 Give unto the Lord, O ye mighty, give unto the Lord glory and strength. 2 Give unto the Lord the glory due unto his name; worship the Lord in the beauty of holiness. 3 The voice of the Lord is upon the waters: the God of glory thundereth: the Lord is upon many waters. 4 The voice of the Lord is powerful; the voice of the Lord is full of majesty."

14 "14 You are the light of the world. A city that is set on a hill cannot be hidden. 15 Nor do they light a lamp and put it under a basket, but on a lampstand, and it gives light to all who are in the house. 16 Let your light so shine before men, that they may see your good works and glorify your Father in heaven."

Chapter Five

Companion Virtue and Potency of Gratitude

> *How that in a great trial of affliction the abundance of their joy and their deep poverty abounded unto the riches of their liberality. (2 Corinthians 8: 2)*

Before attempting to unveil gratitude, we must discuss a serious matter before God – being the true worshippers of the living God. Worshipping God is not merely putting some activities together but the opening of the eyes of our understanding to know Him.[1] Without accepting and responding to grace (knowing God through Christ Jesus),[2] we will find it impossible to live a true life of divine gratitude. It is not all about being God's glorious and redeemed children but being His bond servants by observing and abiding by God's will. For example, Paul defined himself as a bond servant of the Lord[3] and was willing to know God by obeying Him to the letter and abiding by His will, which prompted him to live a life of gratitude because grace found him.[4]

In the context of knowing God, the Bible reveals that the great people of God are primarily characterised by a passion to truly know Him. For example, Moses exclaimed, *"I pray You show me Your glory,"*[5] and David prayed, *"As the deer pants for the water brooks, so my soul pants for You, O God."*[6] Likewise, Paul lamented that his heart yearned to *"know Him and the power of His resurrection and the fellowship of His sufferings."*[7] Our greatest desire or yearning as a true Christian should be to know God. We should constantly be reminded that being a Christian is not possible without really knowing God. [8]

Until we have this revelation and meet God as God, we may likely not be able to express divine gratitude. The potency of gratitude stems from being a worshipper in the knowledge of God,[9] as gratitude is not an act of emotion[10] but a virtue. As believers, we have the onus to be grateful even in the absence of any concomitant emotion. Let me emphasise here again that gratitude is not merely an affective or psychological state, as understood by many today, but a virtue, a lifestyle associated with pure worship.

As gratitude is the beginning of honouring God, and true honouring cannot be attained unless built on a foundation of true worship (humility and obedience); gratefulness is the womb of greatness.

Gratitude is a matter of grace, a complete and humble response to grace, an overflow of abundant grace in our lives. The grace of God sets us free and empowers us to be generous so that others can also receive the grace of God. Gratitude increases generosity. The grace of gratitude that creates generosity surpasses human ability, as divine gratitude, born from the brokenness of the heart, also produces generosity in times of trials.

Gratitude emanates from the spirit, but it can be expressed in various forms. It can be verbally expressed through words of appreciation and encouragement (Psalm 100) or humble acts of service in the sacrificial giving of our time and resources (Colosians.3: 12–15, John 3: 16). Regardless of the form of expression, two certain attributes of translational gratitude are *humility* and *contentment*. Like gratitude, these two virtues are spiritual and stem from the Spirit of God living in the redeemed man. We will take a closer look at these two companion virtues of gratitude to better understand their interrelationship and their implications for our daily lives.

Humility and Gratitude

From a biblical standpoint, gratitude, either in words or deeds, pertains to acknowledging God's sovereignty over and divine providence in the affairs of men. As mentioned in the previous chapter, it is an acknowledgement that all the good gifts we enjoy have been graciously given to us by Him. Hence, gratitude must always be "encased in humility" in the realisation that we are all the undeserving beneficiaries of the grace of a benevolent God. Treading in this consciousness should impact the way we act towards others. Oftentimes, when favours and benefits are extended to us, we act as if we are owed and deserving of the favours and benefits received. Other times, we get so engrossed in enjoying the blessings that we do not take the time to reflect and appreciate the giver. Whenever we are humbly grateful for the favours and benefits received, it attracts more favour. Gratitude expressed in humility always accords an opportunity to request more.

The life of Ruth illustrates this principle (Ruth 1–4). Ruth, through humility and gratitude, progressed from a widowed plantation worker to a high-ranking personality in the society. She humbly submitted to Naomi, her mother-in-law, and found favour with Boaz, her relative and the owner of the plantation where she worked. Boaz eventually redeemed Ruth through marriage in accordance to Jewish customs. Ruth's humility and gratitude grafted her into the lineage of our Lord Jesus Christ despite her Moabite origin, which ordinarily should have disqualified her (Matthew 1: 1–5). Peter Hon Wan Lau in his book *Identity and Ethics in the Book of Ruth* comments that Ruth used her gratitude towards Boaz to humbly request more favours from him.[11] In this regard, I concur with Peter Lau, as my personal experiences with God have also shown me that a heart of gratitude increases favour with God as well as man.

Contentment and Gratitude

When the Word of God calls us to discard all covetousness, it emphatically demands us to "be content." If the antithetical life is saying "no" to sin and "yes" to God, we must say "no" to covetousness and "yes" to contentment. What is contentment? The term "contentment" literally means "to be satisfied" or "to be sufficient."

> To be content is to know that we lack nothing. It is to say, "I have everything that I need." It is to confess like David, "The Lord is my shepherd; I shall not want."

Contentment does not pertain to how much or how little of worldly things we have. In this regard, Paul advises as follows:

Not that I speak in respect of want: for I have learnt, in whatsoever state I am, therewith to be content. I know both how to be abased, and I know how to abound: everywhere and in all things I am instructed both to be full and to be hungry, both to abound and to suffer need. (Philippians 4: 11–12)

A child of God can and does confess contentment regardless of the circumstances of life.

The Bible says that "*godliness with contentment is (a) great gain*" (1 Timothy 6: 6). Godliness means partaking in or showcasing the divine nature of God. We exhibit godliness when we obey and dwell in God's will. Having already established that gratitude (giving thanks) is the will of God for us (1 Thessalonians 5: 16–18), we can, therefore, conclude that gratitude is an integral component of godliness.

1 Timothy 6:6 goes on to show the *incremental effect* of combining godliness (which includes gratitude) with contentment. The following is an extraction from 1 Timothy 6:6 concerning the *incremental effect* of combining godliness (divine gratitude) with contentment (divine humility).

> Godliness (Gratitude) + Contentment (Humility)
> = Great Gain (Exceeding Greatness)[12]

Unveiling Gratitude

Godly contentment is a state of being characterised by satisfaction with who we are and what we have (Matthew 6: 25). However, this does not imply that we should remain stagnant and not aspire to progress or improve in our circumstances and endeavours. Having godly aspirations enables us to successfully discover, diligently develop and effectively deploy our God-given resources. God's will for us is to maximise the potential He has placed in us (Mathew 25: 14–30).

However, godly aspirations should not be confused with ungodly ambition. Ungodly ambition is fuelled by covetousness and greed. It creates an insatiable appetite to acquire more, for the primary purpose of self-gratification or self-aggrandisement. Ungodly ambition eventually leads to destruction; the price paid to achieve an ungodly ambition is often greater than the desired goal. Some may erroneously think that contentment can be attained by relentlessly acquiring more – more money, more power or more of whatever desired. However, contentment cannot be attained by adding to what we have but by subtracting whatever is not in God's will for us from our desires.

To be truly content in life, we must be consciously grateful for the godly inheritance we have as believers in Christ Jesus (Colossians 2: 20, Colossians 3: 3). As believers in Jesus Christ, we have so much to be grateful for, but sometimes, life's constant demands, struggles and worries weigh us down and make us lose sight of how richly blessed we are (Ephesians 1: 3, 2 Peter 1: 3). Amidst life's pressures, we forget to pause and give thanks to God for all He has done for us.

Walking in the virtues of contentment and gratitude gives us the right perspective on life and its challenges. It prevents us from seeing our situation as hopeless because we realise that all things work together for good for those who love God (Romans 8: 28). The secret to contentment is to live daily with an attitude of gratitude.

On the other hand, one of the strategies Satan commonly uses to destroy our act of godliness is stirring up the spirit of discontentment in our heart. Satan used it successfully when he tempted Eve in the Garden of Eden (Genesis 3), by attacking and diminishing her gratitude and contentment potency. The evil provoked Eve to be dissatisfied with God's "order," and he attempts to do the same to us today, to be dissatisfied with God's order or human-constituted order. When our contentment potency is broken, our discontentment is elevated, which comes with terrible consequences – the separation from God's love.

Consequences of Discontentment

> The departure of gratitude marks the automatic arrival of discontentment.

Man's original sin in the Garden of Eden can be described as a form of discontentment. The ungodly ambition to be like God led Adam and Eve into disobedience. Even though God had already granted them dominion to rule over earth (Genesis 1: 28), they became discontented and coveted God's position. Discontentment resulted in the fall of Adam and Eve from grace to spiritual death, marking a shift from a blessed garden of fruitfulness in Eden to a cursed land of toil (Genesis 3: 1–19). As it was in the beginning, so it is now, discontentment always leads to man's downfall. It disconnects us from God and prevents us from receiving favours from God and men.

Just as true gratitude is always accompanied by humility and contentment so does discontentment always coexist with greed, materialism and ungodly ambition.

Many failures in friendships, marriages, businesses and Christian ministry today can be attributed to discontentment. Distinguishing between godly aspiration and ungodly ambition rooted in discontentment requires the grace of God. Oftentimes, we interpret the Scriptures out of context in a bid to fulfil our selfish ambitions. In order to fulfil God's purpose for our lives, we must view our circumstances (where we are and what we have) in the light of God's will for us.

If discontentment is the cause of numerous problems today, then contentment rooted in gratitude is the solution to alleviate the problems.

Potency of Gratitude

Gratitude is one of the vital forces of abundance and fruitfulness. In the biblical account of Jesus feeding five thousand men (John 6: 1–14), He gave thanks for the five loaves of bread and two fish before distributing it to the multitude. His act of expressing gratitude to God for the little boy's lunch caused a supernatural increase that was enough to feed thousands and still be left with twelve baskets of food.

Gratitude is not just an expression of appreciation; it is a lever to unlock strength for the fulfilment of our purpose in life. The Bible says God has already given us all that we need for life and godliness:

> *...as His divine power has given to us all things that pertain to life and godliness, through the knowledge of Him who called us by glory and virtue... (2 Peter 1: 2–4)*

What is required of us is to discover and activate this exceedingly great power at work within us. To do this, we must receive God's words with gratitude because God's divine power is triggered by His words (Genesis 1, John 1: 1–5). When we understand and receive the precious promises in God's Word with gratitude, the joy of the Lord becomes our strength. We become empowered to overcome all challenges in life. The biblical account of Nehemiah rebuilding the broken walls of Jerusalem highlights this point:

9 And Nehemiah, which is the Tirshatha, and Ezra the priest the scribe, and the Levites that taught the people, said unto all the people, This day is holy unto the Lord your God; mourn not, nor weep. For all the people wept, when they heard the words of the law. 10 Then he said unto them, Go your way, eat the fat, and drink the sweet, and send portions unto them for whom nothing is prepared: for this day is holy unto our Lord: neither be ye sorry; for the joy of the Lord is your strength. (Nehemiah 8: 9–10)

The aforementioned statement of Nehemiah grants us an insight into his mindset while rebuilding the broken walls of Jerusalem. He was able to complete the project in record time despite the strong opposition from neighbouring tribes because he refused to allow external occurrences to affect his inner state of being. To Nehemiah, gratitude was like an inner cistern of power, and the joy of the Lord was his strength.

Gratitude re-adjusts our lenses to see situations from God's perspective. Thereby, we receive God's divine strength to overcome all of life's trials. David is another example of a man who understood the potency of gratitude. Many of the most popular thanksgiving psalms/songs we recite today were authored by him (Psalm 8, 42, 100, 103). Therefore, it is not surprising that he was able to surmount numerous challenges and emerge victorious. He defeated a giant (Goliath), survived assassination attempts (from King Saul and Absalom), united the divided tribes of Israel and reigned as king. In David's writings, he often reminded himself to "*bless the Lord, give thanks to the Lord, sing to the Lord and worship the Lord.*"[13] Gratitude was a weapon David used to overcome fear, avoid sadness and access God's supernatural strength for victory.

Nevertheless, permit me to say here that without sound teaching and revelation on gratitude, we and the church stand the risk of losing true committed friends and membership, respectively. Gratitude is important or necessary to all of us because of our social nature and need for nurtured relationships at all levels, whether with God or humanity, within the church or other organisations and the environs, and gratitude is central to all these relationships.

The act or practice of gratitude is important to people, and gratefulness appears to be a highly valued virtue that binds people together,[14] for marriages, family, friends, relationships and the church to experience healthy and successful living. Thus, as individuals and the church, we must seek to not only understand gratitude but also practise, live by it, as this is the *will* of God for His people[15] – fruitfulness.

To successfully win souls for Christ and maintain our personal relationships with others, the potency of gratitude must be a virtue desired by all. It is only through gratitude through the Holy Spirit that we can stand together in unity for divine success as depicted in Psalm 133.[16] Living out gratitude empowers us to stand in unity, overlooking the flaws of others from our human perspective. Incorporating such an attitude and practices into all our relationships will bring about divine unity, togetherness, success, soundness of mind and good health, fruitfulness, dominion and the empowerment to walk in God's revelation according to His command or mandate given to us in Genesis 1: 26–28. This will free us from presumptuous sin and secret faults that can render us both eternally unfit and physically unwell. Regardless of what we go through, gratitude is source of both spiritual and physical healing – a "healing balm."

> Gratitude is not an obligation but an act of benevolence, emanating from a desire to act divinity.

Gratitude – A Healing Balm

Besides the spiritual benefits of gratitude, it also has physical and emotional benefits. A grateful heart is a preventative and therapeutic measure in cardiology (Proverbs 17: 22). Research has shown that when we are grateful, the parasympathetic (calming) part of the nervous system is triggered, decreasing the cortisol levels in the body and reducing the risk of cardiovascular/heart issues.

Gratitude also acts as a natural antidepressant (Matthew 11: 28–29), as it increases the oxytocin levels in the body. Oxytocin is a hormone secreted by the posterior lobe of the pituitary gland located at the base of the brain. It is sometimes known as the "cuddle hormone" or "love hormone," as it is released when people snuggle or bond.

Gratitude inspires and produces holistic health, as it covers the spiritual, psychological and cultural aspects of human life. Today, the practice of gratitude is gaining ground as a therapeutic measure. According to Birnbaum and Friedman,[17] those who practice gratitude are not only happier but also healthier.

Owing to the remarkable healing effect of gratitude, researchers are examining its effects on health outcomes using state-of-the-art biomarkers of health and aging. Clinical trials have shown that the practice of gratitude is associated with lower blood pressure and improved immune function as well as serves as a good sleeping aid, which support the following Bible verse:

> *A merry heart does good, like medicine, But a broken spirit dries the bones. (Proverbs 17: 22)*

When the heart is filled with merriment (gratitude), cardiovascular disease risk factors such as depression, anxiety and substance-abuse disorders are reduced. When our heart is saturated with the spirit of gratitude, it eliminates the thought of suicide. Medically, findings have revealed that gratitude is associated with higher levels of good cholesterol (HDL), lower levels of bad cholesterol (LDL) as well as both systolic and diastolic blood pressure (both at rest and in the face of stress), higher levels of heart rate variability (HRV), a marker of cardiac coherence, lower levels of creatinine (renal functioning). It also lowers the levels of C-reactive protein, a marker of cardiac inflammation indicating heart disease. Thus, gratitude can be considered a medical preventative therapy and a weapon in spiritual warfare.

Consequently, when we recognise God's outpouring love, mercy and favour and respond aptly with gratefulness, gratitude is "born," which is one of the strongest spiritual weapons believers can use to encourage and sustain themselves in the Christian faith.[18] When we compare ourselves to others or complain about issues, we short-change ourselves, rendering ourselves to not only defeats but also health risks, which can have the ultimate effect of making us miserable, leaving us unhappy and impure rather than joyful and pure (Psalm 24 :3–6).

> When we sit down and contemplate deeply with a pure heart, regardless of how bad things may seem to be, we will always find something for which to be thankful, and this brings hope and healing to the soul and spirit

Purity of Heart

One of the most dreaded diseases in the world today is, what we call, "heart disease" or heart trouble. Every day, we hear of people being knocked down by a heart attack or suffering from heart failure. When the heart is in trouble, the rest of the body is in trouble as well. Likewise, when our spiritual heart is in trouble, which leads to a spiritual heart attack or heart failure, we are disconnected from God's truth, and the remaining parts of our body suffer a spiritual attack, yielding and succumbing to our thoughts, motives and desires instead of God. Our heart needs to be pure to produce godly gratitude.

The state of our heart plays an important role in expressing godly gratitude. As gratitude stems from the heart, the heart must be in connection and partnership with God's will. The Lord Jesus said, *"Blessed are the pure in heart, for they shall see God."*[19]

Pride slays the purity of the heart, but a pure heart is the soil from which gratitude naturally springs and creates an atmosphere for increase.

The purity of heart is a matter of motive and desire, and our motive and desire should be God and His righteousness. To pursue the purity of heart, God and His righteousness must be our ultimate goals. We were created for God's glory and to proclaim His praises. We will be able to do so only when our heart is right [20] and we are appreciative of God's purpose for our life. We exist to worship God and lead a genuine life, so worship must come from a pure heart. Such worship must be an expression of our real feelings – adoring God above everything else, submitting to His every command. It is God's plan that we all *"be conformed to the likeness of His Son."* (Romans 8: 29), which begins with a heart of gratitude for what God has done for us. This thought enables us to strive towards having a pure heart, conforming us to God's likeness and purpose.

To be pure in heart means to seek only God and His righteousness, and this, according to Jesus, makes us see God. Our motives, intentions, desires and purposes must emanate from a pure heart to be able to worship God and lead a life of gratitude. Therefore, having a pure heart means that our heart is focused on a single goal, seeking nothing but the Lord Jesus Christ. In other words, our desires, thoughts, and decisions must pertain to seeking only God Himself, and our heart should not be troubled for anything else, as Jesus said, *"let not your heart be troubled"* (John 14: 1–3). To avoid "heart trouble," we must attune our spirit and heart to God's frequency. We need to adjust to accommodate God's will to have a clean spirt and pure heart; otherwise, we may find it difficult to experience the pure life and gratitude of the Kingdom.

Unveiling Gratitude

More so, in John 14, Jesus' reference is not to physical heart trouble but a spiritual heart illness that lures us away from God's purpose and the truth of our existence – a troubled heart, a corrupt heart, a burdened heart and a sorrowful heart produced by focusing on human motives, desires or wants,[21] which can prevent us from having a pure heart, thus making living a life of gratitude difficult. When our inward condition (heart) towards the Lord is pure, an eternal joy that produces peace will spontaneously emerge as the outward state, expressing the likeness of God.

> Unveiling gratitude is unveiling the purity of the heart towards God. God is more pleased with a heart of gratitude than music produced by angelic voices.

Certainly, to avoid a spiritual heart problem, we should not only seek peace, joy, physical or spiritual blessings but also set our heart upon God, as our goal and motive. With this mindset, we will be able to live a life of gratitude and peace amidst the conflicts and trials of life. When our heart is pure, it attains peace. Thus, the night before Jesus died, He gave His peace to us (John 14: 27).[22]

Having a pure heart entails allowing God's Kingdom to take birth in you, which is expressed in Matthew 6: 10 as *"Thy Kingdom come."* For God's Kingdom to come, we must be poor in *spirit*, and to be poor in *spirit* is to have a pure heart. The Kingdom does not come in an external way but in an internal way. The Kingdom comes from within our spirit and heart, so our heart must be pure and poor in spirit.

Despite asking God's Kingdom to come, failing to see any spiritual manifestation of its presence can be due to a heart problem – not being poor in our spirit to receive Christ or not having a pure heart towards God and His purpose. The coming of God's Kingdom is Christ growing, dwelling and reigning permanently within us. When this happens, gratitude becomes a lifestyle.

Understanding God's purpose for our life gravitates us towards being grateful not just for physical reasons but also for being in conformity with God purpose, which empowers us to express gratitude.

> Taking for granted all the temporal provisions and spiritual blessings that God has so richly bestowed on us, and so failing to continually give thanks is one of our "acceptable sins." – Jerry Bridges[23]

Essence of Gratitude

Spiritual gratitude means expressing gratitude from God's viewpoint, which is embedded in having the mind of Christ. While basic gratitude is passively triggered by external positive factors, such as achievements and possessions, spiritual (Christ-centred or godly) gratitude is internalised, deliberately patterned and directed towards God's will as well as exercised and expressed in all circumstances to reveal and glorify no one but God. Hence, a godly gratitude is never dependent on changing conditions but on the mind of Christ that is within us (Philippians 2: 5–8).[24]

Paul's instruction, *"Let this mind be in you"* and *"…who being in the form of God, did not consider it robbery*[25] *to be equal with God"* (Philippians 2: 6), reveals that Jesus was willing to give up *his life* as well as be obedient and submissive to His Father. For unveiling, the flesh has to be separated from the spirit,[26] to allow the will of God to prevail, as we wrestle against principalities, powers and wickedness.[27]

Jesus readily gave up the full glory of God to become a human, willingly committing to be the sacrifice for all human sin. The most interesting aspect for us to emulate from Jesus is His confident acceptance of God's plan for Him, despite knowing its repercussions for Him. He knew what God's plan was, placed confidence in the plan and agreed with the plan. This means that Jesus knew the mind of His Father, and the Father knew His. As

Unveiling Gratitude

Jesus knew the mind of God and the mind of God was in Him, Jesus was spiritually disciplined and mature to live out gratitude despite the humiliating circumstance. A proper or in-depth understanding of who we are and what surrounds us gives us a sound mind[28] to live in God's plan without fear and be filled with exceeding gratitude.

To establish a good relationship with God and express godly gratitude, we must have the same mind and attitude as Jesus, which include consolation, humility, obedience, comfort, fellowship, affection and love. Having the mind of Christ helps build in us the spiritual desire to be spiritually disciplined and the maturity to express God's nature and purpose in any circumstance – being grateful, the will of God for us (1 Thessalonians 5: 18).

> Gratitude to God should be as habitual as the reception of mercies is constant, as ardent as the number of them is great, as devout as the riches of divine grace and goodness is incomprehensible.
> – Simmons[29]

Basic gratitude is a set of momentary and mutable feelings, whereas matured spiritual gratitude is an expressive action. Spiritual gratitude is not only experienced but also expressed, revealing the very nature of God. The spiritual gratitude is practised not only because it feels good but also because it's the right thing to do. It is practised for not one's own good but for the good of others – one's family, church, work, business, community and society. The maturity of gratitude is, in fact, not a feeling at all but a spiritual virtue.

> Epicurus says, "gratitude is a virtue that commonly has profit annexed to it." And where is the virtue that has not? But still the virtue is to be valued for itself, and not for the profit that attends it.
> – Seneca[30]

Completeness

The intent of gratitude is not to seek profit; however, living in gratitude is a great gain on its own, as it gives contentment to the body, soul and spirit (1 Timothy 6: 6).[31] Gratitude brings out the broken and renewed man in us, outward from the inward, empowering us to appreciate God's realities outside ourselves. Unveiled gratitude exposes and brings us to the state and maturity of understanding that we are incomplete on our own human dimensional level. God through His grace has placed us in a *spiritual web* of interconnected relationships to make us *complete*. This means gratitude humbles us to see in others what we lack. As we become appreciative of God's grace, we automatically become complete through Christ,[32] who also lives in them (others), by grace to showcase God's wonders because of His covenant with man.[33]

From all eternity, God through His grace and mercy has reconciled us to Himself, for making us "complete" and aligning our mission with His purpose, and He does this through a covenant relationship.

> When gratitude is insulated in God's Word, it becomes a stream that circulates our mindfulness, building greater capacity attitude amongst nothing for something exceedingly great.

When the human spirit lacks peace and rest, the tendency to not appreciate the God's grace hovering above and overflowing around us through other people arise in us, making us react to every situation negatively. When we are matured in our act of gratitude, it empowers us to appreciate and affirm the worth and value of other people, structures and systems as well as the supernatural powers of God manifesting around us, rather than taking them for granted and abusing the grace of God made available to us to live in dominion, reflecting His likeness and glory.

Unveiling Gratitude

Gratitude ultimately doesn't depend on the circumstances that seem inevitable or difficult to control; rather, it depends on the perspective and attitude we hold. For example, Mary, the mother of Jesus, was filled with gratitude regarding God's plan through her despite hard circumstances, but her perspective, reaction and acceptance of God's grace saw her through the controversial situation God's "purpose" placed her in (Luke 1: 26–38). When we embrace God's plan and purpose (*act of being grateful*), He surrounds us with the supernatural power to achieve exceeding greatness. When gratitude is unveiled, God's plan and purpose for our life are established and His prophetic words, decrees and blessings are activated, for the world to see His glory through us.

In conclusion, stating a personal conviction and not generalising, by God's grace, I believe I speak the heart of the Scriptures when I say the negligence of expressing genuine gratitude for any form of beneficence to the benefactor, whoever they may be, is regarded as arrogance and the denial of humility,[34] and one who fails to do so is an enemy of the Cross.[35] While humility[36] is the producer of all virtues, gratitude is a spinoff of humility.[37] Unveiling gratitude is living in Christ's humility and likeness to bring others to the Cross in order to see and encounter Jesus for their salvation and redemption.

Therefore, ensure you live a life of gratitude so that you can be a special gift to someone by playing a role in making their life fulfilled. As Jesus is a gift to the world, you are a gift unto the world. Unveil gratitude by being humble, thankful, grateful and appreciative that God gave you a life, regardless of the circumstance you find yourself.

The circumstances in which we find ourselves are never the reasons for our lack of gratitude or thankfulness but the lack of our understanding of the circumstances. Jesus was faced with a challenging circumstance, but He overcame it because He understood the *will*[38] of the Father regarding the "circumstance" and was grateful, as His circumstance was to give life and give it abundantly. A heart of gratitude is a heart of praise. Give praise to God, not necessarily for what we have been given but because of who God is and what He has done in totality – the visible and invisible.

> Grace-mindedness is the purest source of gratitude. Acknowledging and applying God's abiding grace to your life and applying the same to others as an appreciation for God's benevolence make you blessed amongst men.

In every circumstance, we are to "doxologicalise"[39] the Lord to unveil gratitude so that others may see His glory through our praise. Doxology is an offering of praise to God in worship, exalting God, from whom *all* blessings emanate and life flows. Knowing about the Lord is meaningless without doxological expression; worship and praise –acts of unveiling gratitude – and give glory in the highest form to the "most high God."[40]

Divinely, gratitude is far deeper than the surface words we verbalise or our bodily and attitudinal expressions. It is an internal praise that erupts like a volcanic flame, unveiling the hidden potency of the thankfulness and appreciation that lie at the bedrock of the heart, the inner man. A heart of gratitude speaks of a lived life of doxology, a life of praise – reflective praise.[41] A lived life of doxology entails praising God when we feel like there's no reason to praise God.[42]

What is the doxology of gratitude, practice and living?

Endnotes

1 Ephesians 1: 18

2 Philippians 3: 10 – "That I may know Him and the power of His resurrection, and the fellowship of His sufferings, being conformed to His death."

3 Romans 1: 1 – "Paul, a bondservant of Jesus Christ, called to be an apostle, separated to the gospel of God."

4 1 Corinthians 15: 7–10 – "9 For I am the least of the apostles, who am not worthy to be called an apostle, because I persecuted the church of God. 10 But by the grace of God I am what I am, and His grace toward me was not in vain; but I laboured more abundantly than they all, yet not I, but the grace of God which was with me."

5 Exodus 33: 17–18 – "17 So the Lord said to Moses, 'I will also do this thing that you have spoken; for you have found grace in My sight, and I know you by name'. 18 And he said, 'Please, show me Your glory'."

6 Psalm 42: 1 – "As the deer [b]pants for the water brooks, So pants my soul for You, O God."

7 Philippians 3: 10 – "That I may know Him and the power of His resurrection, and the fellowship of His sufferings, being conformed to His death."

8 John 14: 8–9 – "8 Philip said to Him, 'Lord, show us the Father, and it is sufficient for us'. 9 Jesus said to him, 'Have I been with you so long, and yet you have not known Me, Philip? He who has seen Me has seen the Father; so how can you say, "Show us the Father"'?"

9 Ephesians 1: 17–18 – "17 that the God of our Lord Jesus Christ, the Father of glory, may give to you the spirit of wisdom and revelation in the knowledge of Him, 18 the eyes of your [a] understanding being enlightened; that you may know what is the hope of His calling, what are the riches of the glory of His inheritance in the saints."

10 It is also important to understand the role of passion in the exercise of virtue. The emotion or passion referred to here is love in obedience to God's will and not some negative emotions due to circumstantial problems, as we are to give thanks in every circumstance. Passion is the root of all virtues.

11 Peter Hon Wan Lau, Identity and Ethics in the Book of Ruth: A Social Identity Approach (Walter de Gruyter & Co., 2010).

12 Genesis 26: 1–14: Isaac's obedience (gratitude and humility) to dwell in Gerar secured him Great Gain – exceeding greatness, which 1 Timothy 6: 6 expresses as "Godliness (gratitude) with Contentment (humility) is a great gain." Obedience is a combination of gratitude and humility, which produces meekness. The great gain of the meek is to that "they will inherit the earth" (Matthew 5: 5).

13 Psalm 30: 4, Psalm 103, Psalm 66: 8, Psalm 68: 19m, Psalm 43: 4, Psalm 144: 9. Psalm 147: 7, 1 Chronicles 29: 10-13. Christians are exhorted to praise God in every situation. David was always grateful. He lived a life of gratitude. David's gratitude was well noted in his expressing adoration and respect to God, not only in repeated and ritualistic speech but in attitude and lifestyle.

14 Binds people together here means living in unity, which only comes about by expressing gratitude. One of the potencies of gratitude is unity, which is expressed in Psalm 133.

15 1 Thessalonians 5: 18

16 "1 Behold, how good and how pleasant it is For brethren to dwell together in unity! 2 It is like the precious oil upon the head, Running down on the beard, The beard of Aaron, Running down on the edge of his garments. 3 It is like the dew of Hermon, Descending upon the mountains of Zion; For there the Lord commanded the blessing — Life forevermore."

17 T.H Birnbaum & H.H. Friedman, "Gratitude and Generosity" (2014: 6).

18 Gratitude is the most unexploited spiritual weapon. Often, we don't even realise gratitude is a spiritual weapon. Romans 1: 21 – "Because although they knew God, they did not glorify Him as God, nor were thankful, but became futile in their thoughts, and their foolish hearts were darkened."

19 Matthew 5: 8

20 1 Corinthians 10: 31, Ephesians 1: 11–12, 1 Peter 2: 9

21 Our heart trouble can be due to our wants, sicknesses, unfruitfulness, pain, lack of money, among others.

22 "Peace I leave with you, My peace I give to you; not as the world gives do I give to you. Let not your heart be troubled, neither let it be afraid."

23 Jerry Bridges, Respectable Sins: Confronting the Sins We Tolerate (Tyndale House, Colorado Springs, CO., 2014) pp. 30–56.

24 "Let this mind be in you which was also in Christ Jesus, 6 who, being in the form of God, did not consider it robbery to be equal with God, 7 but made Himself of no reputation, taking the form of a bondservant, and coming in the likeness of men. 8 And being found in appearance as a man, He humbled Himself

and became obedient to the point of death, even the death of the cross."

25 Robbery, in this context, means something to be held onto or grasped at.

26 Galatians 5: 17 – This verse reveals the antithesis between the flesh and the spirit; the flesh desires to puff up, but the spirit desires to be humbled in God's will, unveiling gratitude to behold God's glory.

27 Ephesians 6: 12 – "For we do not wrestle against flesh and blood, but against principalities, against powers, against the rulers of the darkness of this age, [a] against spiritual hosts of wickedness in the heavenly places."

28 2 Timothy 1: 7: "For God has not given us a spirit of fear, but of power and of love and of a sound mind. Having a sound mind of who we are in Christ us makes us to fall in line with God's purpose willingly."

29 Tryon Edwards, The New Dictionary of Thoughts: A Cyclopedia of Quotations (Literary Licensing, LLC, 2012).

30 Tryon Edwards, The New Dictionary of Thoughts: A Cyclopedia of Quotations (Literary Licensing, LLC, 2012).

31 Now, godliness with contentment is a great gain. Contentment here signifies gratitude.

32 Colossians 2: 7–12

33 Hebrews 13: 20–21 – Complete here means an ongoing process of repairing brokenness, restoring damage, reconciling separation, reorienting the knocked askew, rearranging or reequipping.

34 Proverbs 8: 13, James 4: 16, Psalm 36: 11, Jeremiah 48: 29, 2 Timothy 3: 2

35 Philippians 3: 18–19 – "18 For many walk, of whom I have told you often, and now tell you even weeping, that they are the enemies of the cross of Christ: 19 Whose end is destruction, whose God is their belly, and whose glory is in their shame, who mind earthly things."

36 Humility in its essence is Christlikeness. Humility is the putting on and exhibiting of the "likeness." Humility is *unveiling gratitude*. Philippians 2: 3–5 – "3 Let nothing be done through strife or vainglory; but in lowliness of mind let each esteem other better than themselves. 4 Look not every man on his own things, but every man also on the things of others. 5 Let this mind be in you, which was also in Christ Jesus."

37 Philippians 2: 8 – "And being found in fashion as a man, he humbled himself, and became obedient unto death, even the death of the cross."

38 Luke 22: 42 – "Saying, Father, if thou be willing, remove this cup from me: nevertheless not my will, but thine, be done." Read Luke 22: 40–60

39 Doxologicalise here means to praise the Lord. It is an expression of giving praise to God. It can be done through performing a deed or gesture or singing praise to the worthiness of God. The word doxologicalise is coined from doxology and doxological. Doxology gives comfort and assurance that God is all faithful and truthful to His words. There is doxology as praise (1 Chronicles 29: 10–13, Psalm 72: 18–19, Psalm 106: 48) and doxology as benediction (Luke 1: 68–79, Romans 15: 5–6, 2 Corinthians 13: 14)

40 Psalm 57: 2 – "I will cry unto God most high; unto God that performeth all things for me."

41 Job 42: 2 – Job here demonstrated a kind of reflective praise, where he thought of God's greatness.

42 For example, Paul and David were persecuted, embarrassed, mocked, beaten, imprisoned and made public criminals, but they died to live a life worthy of Christ – a life of praise.

Chapter Six

Doxology of Gratitude – In All Things Give Thanks

At this juncture, I am inspired to write an epilogue on the imperativeness to give thanks to God in all things. Yes, we need to give thanks to God in all things and in everything by the will of God. This is also a cardinal commandment of God according to the Scriptures. In 1 Thessalonians 5: 18, the Bible aptly reveals the mind of God on the sublime subject of gratitude: *"We are all enjoined to give thanks in everything."* It is the will of God in Christ Jesus concerning us all that we show gratitude in all situations and circumstances of our lives, seeing that God is graciously reconciled to us in Christ Jesus in whom now live, move and have our being. Moreover, through His merciful reconciliation, He has given us great reasons to rejoice evermore and appointed us in all things to give thanks, as it is delightful and pleasing to Him. It is the spirit of grace and humility that assists us in our prayers and expressions of thanksgiving. In this equation, humility is our spiritual springboard as well as our watchword. It is easier for a humble person to cultivate the presence of mind to give thanks to his maker and appreciate and show gratitude to his fellow human beings where and when the contexts and circumstances require. In this line of thought, Alistair Begg has made the following disclosure and statements on humility:

> The Bible does not call us to "feel humble" but to adopt an attitude of lowliness. This lowliness is like a garment that reveals itself in servant hood. We should not leave home without it. When the garment of humility is absent, friendships are marred, families are broken, and fellowships are destroyed.[1]

Dr Mark Amadi

I concur with Alistair Begg regarding his thoughts on the relationship between our acts of humility and fellowship. Fellowship is important to God, and anything that poses a threat to it constitutes a sin in God's eye. Ingratitude involves an infringement of our fellowship with God and, therefore, is an act of sin. Gratitude is a vital part of our Christian service to God. We must obey all biblical injunctions regarding our being thankful at all times. Any genuine Christian will say he or she wants to serve and obey God. But we disobey God when we refuse and neglect to serve Him accordingly. Failing to serve God in total obedience is sinful.

Our acts of gratitude are passionately linked to our acts of obedience. What this means is that we must be truly and faithfully motivated by obedience in all our worship and due service to God, as instructed by Moses in the Old Testament:

> *Ye shall walk after the Lord your God, and fear him, and keep his commandments, and obey his voice, and ye shall serve him, and cleave unto him. (Deuteronomy 13:4)*

Everything in the aforementioned scriptural verse pertains to the obedience to God. Moreover, amidst this cluster of biblical injunctions on obedience is the command, "serve him," which is strictly directive and must be obeyed. We must serve God because we want to do His bidding in obedience. We must by all means avoid sinning against God so that we can prosper and do well in life. We must praise Him constantly and be thankful at all times and in all seasons. Our humble praise–prayer (doxology) must be *"Oh Lord we praise thee and give all glory to thee. Amen."*[2]

> Gratitude unveils our hidden treasures and reveals our hidden strengths. It turns our nothingness into something. It turns scarcity into surplus and mourning into joy.

Apostle Paul, the inspired author of the first Epistle to the Thessalonians, was overtly delighted at Timothy's good news that the Thessalonian Christian brethren had been tested and proven faithful in discipleship. He also testified that they had received superlative grace and courage to endure and overcome the most gruesome persecutions with which they had been tested. They stood resolute and continued steadfastly in evangelism and the propagation of Christ's saving gospel. It was against this background and a few other doctrinal matters that Apostle Paul joyfully wrote to congratulate the Thessalonian converts and encourage them further to give thanks to the almighty God in all things accordingly. It was apparent that if the Thessalonian converts and disciples could survive and overcome such atrocious persecution, then they must be prepared at all times and in all circumstances to give thanks to God. This is the right and reasonable thing to do. The converts must understand and retain the correct view of God.

To "retain" here means to get the idea settled in our consciousness that God deserves our gratitude at all times. The pertinent question here now is as follows: If we refuse and/or neglect to be the grateful servants of Christ who died for us and saved us, in whom we have access to all things, what then will make us grateful?

Cultivating Faith and Gratitude

To have faith is to believe and act on the Word of God. To express gratitude is to be sincerely thankful to God, the author of His Word. "Word" here is the common denominator and the key spiritual link between the manifesting expressions of our faith and gratitude. To be grateful is to be thankful; to be thankful is to be in the will of God; to be in the will of God is to be in the right standing with God; to be in the right standing with God is to be in God's righteousness; to be in the right standing with God is to be listed in the Book of Life; to be listed in the Book of Life is to be an accredited candidate to heaven.

How do we then cultivate faith and gratitude? We cultivate faith by dwelling and acting on God's word, by trusting Him on the basis on His promises, by keeping His commandments in full and unfeigned obedience, by yielding to the dictates and lead of the Holy spirit and by being filled with the Holy Spirit. When we are filled with the Holy Spirit, we operate under the guardianship of God Himself and our safety is guaranteed. This will then inspire us to cultivate a heart of thankfulness to God, who keeps and secures us. God showers benefits and blessings on us daily. He redeemed and saved us. We have no reason to be unthankful to Him. God created us for His pleasure. It is His good pleasure that we be thankful at all times and in all things.

> Gratitude empowers and enlightens the eye to see light in darkness; it turns an obstacle into an opportunity and pushes the cloud of discouragement far into the ocean.

Where does gratitude come from, and what does God tell us in this regard? As we are created in God's image, we are the partakers in His gracious nature. Therefore, it will be appropriate to imagine that God created us with our wonderful nature to be grateful unless we choose to act otherwise. Hence, it is against the nature and plan of God to be unthankful or ungrateful. It is also correct and appropriate to warn that all ungrateful souls risk the doom of hell fire and eternal damnation. Ingratitude provokes the wrath of God. It bleeds the heart of God and invokes His judgement.

Donald S. Whitney, in his book *Spiritual Disciplines for the Christian Life,* insists that we must be motivated by gratitude at all times. He notes that the prophet Samuel exhorted the people of God to partake in service with the following words of wisdom:

> *Only fear the Lord, and serve him in truth with all your heart: for consider how great things he hath done for you. (1 Samuel 12: 24)*

Whitney further states that serving God is no burden when we consider the numerous great things He has done for us.[3] The grace and privilege He accorded us to know Christ and become saved are crucial here. Moreover, He showed us the mercy to experience true forgiveness and deliverance from eternal damnation from judgment and hell fire. The ultimate assurance of heaven and eternal life in Christ has become our eternal hope. We are able to conclude here that God has never done anything greater for humanity than bring us in love to Himself. The Gospel of John 15: 13 states that *"Greater love hath no man than this that a man lay down his life for his friends."* The relevant question here now is the following: If we refuse and/or neglect being the grateful servants of Christ who died for us and saved us, in whom we have access to all things, what then will make us grateful?

Gratitudinal Thankfulness (Luke 17: 11–19)

In this part of the reflections on the subject of thankfulness, I aim to ponder about the lessons and precepts one can derive from the biblical story of ten lepers as narrated in the Gospel of Luke 17:11–19. The ten lepers encountered a spectacular and special miracle of healing through Christ, the healer Himself. That day was probably the happiest of their lives. Ten of them approached Christ desperately seeking the urgent help of healing and deliverance from the reproachable disease of leprosy. Christ, the merciful King, obliged them and cleansed them wholly. One of the lepers was a Samaritan, and the other nine were Jews. However, the lesson of practical gratitude was exhibited only by the Samaritan leper who was healed. He gratefully returned to Christ to thank Him:

> *11 And it came to pass, as he went to Jerusalem that he passed through the midst of Samaria and Galilee .12 And as he entered into a certain village, there met him ten men that were lepers, which stood afar off. 13 And they lifted up their voices, and said, Jesus, Master, have mercy on us. 14 And when he saw them, he said unto*

> *them, Go shew yourselves unto the priests. And it came to pass, that, as they went, they were cleansed. 15 And one of them, when he saw that he was healed, turned back, and with a loud voice glorified God, 16 And fell down on his face at his feet, giving him thanks: and he was a Samaritan. 17 And Jesus answering said, Were there not ten cleansed? But where are the nine? 18 There are not found that returned to give glory to God, save this stranger. 19 And he said unto him, Arise, go thy way: thy faith hath made thee whole. (Luke 17: 11–19)*

Historically, the miracle of the ten lepers in Luke's narrative under review happened on Jesus' last pilgrimage to Jerusalem where He was to die outside the city wall. He was in transit through Samaria and the Galilee districts when the ten lepers approached Him for help to heal them and He healed them. But Jesus received thanksgiving only from the least expected, a total stranger, a Samaritan. The other nine lepers were Jews who bolted as soon as they were healed. What a shame! Christ Himself commented that none returned "save this stranger." Jesus asked, "Were there not ten cleansed, but where are the nine?" This is a million-dollar question. Why did the nine not return to show gratitude?

Ingratitude is a common and serious sin. We all need help to overcome the monster of ingratitude. Very many of us have received countless mercies from God, but only a few of us have returned to testify and give thanks. It was saddening to learn in this narrative that only a Samaritan and stranger mustered the courage and took the responsibility to make his way back to Jesus to thank Him. We who have received mercy, love, grace, forgiveness and salvation from God must not lose sight of the need to thank Him. We must all come to Him with the most grateful hearts. An ungrateful soul cannot please God. We must reciprocate Christ's love in our attitude of gratitude. We must let our gratitude be our strength of character. Our attitude of gratitude is of great value in the eyes of God. Through a total stranger, a Samaritan, the golden object of gratitude was unveiled.

Besides, in the above pericope, amongst other pericopes, I believe Apostle Luke's intention was for us to understand and accept God's grace for seeing, hearing and responding to His Grace (Jesus Christ),[4] which has been given to us freely through the resurrected Christ. The pericope of the ten lepers creates in us that awareness that we are amongst the ten lepers, who constantly receive mercy and deliverance from God through the risen Christ, who is always present to help in times of our various troubles (Psalm 46: 1).[5] Owing to such an abundance of great love and mercy shown to us by God, He expects us to always come back to Him as the Samaritan with a happy mind – an action of responding to God's unmerited favour with an overflowing heart of gratitude and thankfulness, thereby unveiling the golden object of gratitude. God wants us to be the golden object of gratitude.

The doxology of gratitude of the Samaritan was expressed, performed or rendered by him giving glory (praise) to God and reverencing God by falling on his knees in worship for the mercy received. This Samaritan, a stranger, teaches us in this pericope that gratitude is more than just expressing our thankfulness for what God has done for us through mere words or gesticulations but entails total reverence to Him.[6] The Samaritan has unveiled to us that God considers thankfulness and gratitude to be serious and keeps record of our thankfulness. Thanksgiving, a lifestyle of gratitude, is a pivotal and essential concept in the Scriptures, as it unveils God's will for us – to be thankful in all situations (1 Thessalonians 5: 18).

Nothing pushes us to become bitter, selfish, dissatisfied people more quickly than possessing an ungrateful heart. Oftentimes, sin, anger, jealousy, envy, hatred, unhealthy competition, pride, complaining and a host of others evils spring to life from an unthankful and ingrate heart, which prevents us from giving thanks to

God in circumstances as He wants us to (1 Thessalonians 5: 18). Gratitude eliminates the settling of sin and empowers us to focus on God's intent for us. Gratitude shapes and aligns us with the will of the Father – to worship Him in truth and spirit – where there is of sin, unfaithfulness, unthankfulness or ingratitude.

> True gratitude is a sacrifice of love and not just a verbal expression of a barrage of good words uttered from our comfort zone.

In addition, it is clear at this point that nothing can be more beneficial to restoring the contentment and joy of our salvation than a true spirit of thankfulness, which becomes a living doxology we sing around, as we unveil gratitude in *Gloria in excelsis Deo*,[7] giving God glory in the highest.[8] This means expressing biblical gratitude is an act of holiness, reverencing God for not just what He has done for us but who He is and what He has made us to be when we received Christ into our lives, Royal Priesthood, whose duty or commission is to sing and proclaim His praise;[9] doing His will, which is expressed in our love for Him.[10][11][12]

As I mentioned, gratitude is spiritual in nature and not a philosophical psychological construct or norm for social living. The act and practice of gratitude are means to truly express our love and loyalty to God for not only what He has done but also who He is. To express gratitude to God, the love for God is paramount. This means all our emotions and actions should be directed towards God:

> *37 Jesus said unto him, Thou shalt love the Lord thy God with all thy heart, and with all thy soul, and with all thy mind. 38 This is the first and great commandment. 39 And the second is like unto it, Thou shalt love thy neighbour as thyself. 40 On these two commandments hang all the law and the prophets. (Matthew 22: 37–40)*

Unveiling Gratitude

The above pericope unveils that without love for God, the external observance of the commandments becomes an empty act. This implies that our gratitudinal message and lifestyle – accepting and responding to God's grace – are strictly based on our heart of true love. Unveiling gratitude entails demonstrating our love and loyalty to God in the highest.

Thus, loving God involves being cleansed inside first, for which Christ has come to us through His birth, death and resurrection. Only by possessing a clean hand and pure heart can our obedience be genuine to God, which is revealed in our act and expression of gratitude and thankfulness. The Samaritan could return to show his appreciation to Jesus because he was not only cleansed of leprosy but also cleansed inside, which ignited his love for God and gratitude for what He has done for him. The only way to express his love, faith and gratitude was to go in search of Jesus in order to express how thankful and grateful he was over the healing he received.

Sometimes, when we only verbalise our thanksgiving without true corresponding love for God, we can appear to others to be righteous, but our obedience is corrupted by negative motives, which sinks us deeper into sin. Jesus said that loving God is the first and greatest commandment (Matthew 22: 36–40).[13] For gratitude to be true, divine love must exist, and this, which is the greatest commandment, represents the crux of all the commandments. Understanding here that *love* does not replace all the commandments is imperative, as it is the engine of all other commandments (Exodus 20). Loving God requires faith. Entering and maintaining perfect relationships require faith in the value of the connections. Therefore, to unveil gratitude, faith and the practice of faith are essential. Abraham's practice of faith emanated from his love for God, exhibited and expressed in his act of gratitude by obeying God's will, Word, which prompted him to willingly offer his *only* covenanted son for sacrifice.[14] God counted Abraham's belief[15] in Him as righteousness.[16]

> In every situation, we must learn to thank God, for He is ever present in our dark places. When we think all hope is lost, God is in the situation, awaiting us to see Him working wonders. Sometimes maintaining an attitude of thanksgiving can be difficult because it requires active faith. Having faith in God empowers us to wait patiently on the LORD[17] with a gladsome heart of praise.

Faith is an essential ingredient of love to express gratitude. It takes faith to love, and the eyes of faith to see God's greatness amidst tribulations to be thankful. Loving God and expressing gratitude should not based on situation ethics,[18] as the Scripture says:

> *In everything give thanks: for this is the will of God in Christ Jesus concerning you. (1 Thessalonians 5)*

Faith and love give us the right motive to genuinely obey God's commandments so that our gratitude and thankfulness can be genuine before God. For example, Cain's thanksgiving, offering or sacrifice was rejected by God (Genesis 4: 3–5). God rejected Cain's sacrifice – thanksgiving – because he was lacking in faith (Hebrews 11: 4).[19] Faith is born out of love and the appreciation of who God is. Although some may attribute God's rejection of Cain's offering to His sovereign choice or Cain's offering not being a blood offering,[20] the perusal of Hebrew 11: 4 negates this notion.

Our doxology of gratitude can be rejected when our gratitude is expressed based on our presumption and not by faith. Faith is not merely a feeling of confident expectation, but it is spiritual in nature; it is the result of submitting our body, mind, spirit to God's Word and acting in accordance with His instructions. Our doxology of gratitude must be expressed in the love and respect for the Lord God, which Cain lacked.

Unveiling Gratitude

The doxology of gratitude is a spiritual sacrifice made to God and *must* not have any defects (Malachi 1: 8).[21] Gratitude is not presumptuous but spiritual and intentional in accordance to God's will. God does not respect presumptuousness, about which David lamented:

> *Keep back thy servant also from presumptuous sins; let them not have dominion over me: then shall I be upright, and I shall be innocent from the great transgression. (Psalm 19:13)*

God expects the best from us. When we give God the best, He accepts our doxology and, in turn, blesses us.

> True gratitude is the bridge that helps one cross over to dine with kings and queens, tackle one's chief enemy and makes God glad to open the floodgates of heaven upon one.

Consequently, when gratitude is expressed with a wrong motive, we commit presumptuous sin. A presumptuous spirit doesn't take God's command seriously and embraces situation ethics rather than acting on God's instructional truth. The failure to act in accordance with His command makes our sacrifice defective. God demands and expects a blemish-free sacrifice from us. Thus, to be like the Samaritan who returned to Jesus with appreciation, our act of gratitude must be without blemishes or wrong motives.

Expressing our doxology of gratitude means that everything we do must be done by giving gratitude and thanks to God and all that we do must be for pleasing God the Father. Thus, I conclude here that that our redeemed lifestyle of loving God through faith should be appropriately punctuated by responses of thanks and glory to God, which is classified as doxological. The doxology of gratitude results in response to God's glorious work on our behalf. Our doxology of gratitude can only be performed by dwelling in God's presence and sharing His nature and glory. In other words, according to Peter Brunner,[22] doxology is "nothing but a reflection of God's glory." When we accept and respond to God's grace by living out God's will and exhibiting His gloriousness, we become a living doxology, singing our praise aloud through our acts and deeds, announcing and proclaiming God to those who are yet to gain access to God's glory.

The doxology of gratitude presents us to the world as the light and salt of the world, giving the world a reason to seek God:

> *13 Ye are the salt of the earth: but if the salt have lost his savour, wherewith shall it be salted? It is thenceforth good for nothing, but to be cast out, and to be trodden under foot of men. 14 Ye are the light of the world. A city that is set on a hill cannot be hid. 15 Neither do men light a candle, and put it under a bushel, but on a candlestick; and it giveth light unto all that are in the house. 16 Let your light so shine before men, that they may see your good works, and glorify your Father which is in heaven. (Matthew 5:13–16)*

A closer look at the above periscope unveils that the doxology of gratitude entails far more than mere verbal expression. It involves praising God by our actions, becoming the presence of God to the world after being crucified with Christ, as the flesh (the dead) cannot praise but only the living (the resurrected), those standing in God's will.[23]

Hence, the doxology of gratitude can only be performed where God's glory exists. Eric Peterson explains that the *glory*[24] of God is only found in the resurrected and glorified body of Jesus Christ,[25] who dwells in us, and we carry about[26] when we fully accept and respond to grace.

The performance of the doxology of gratitude is a unique feature of Christian faith. It distinguishes us from the world, as we become a living sacrifice of praise unto the Lord (Romans 12: 1–2). Our lifestyle of gratitude is, therefore, rightly regarded as the epitome of orthodoxy, the correct performance of doxology of gratitude to God.

The act of expressing gratitude involves us in the central mystery of our divine service, which is centred on the physical assumption of Jesus into glory, as reminded by Paul reminded in 1 Timothy 3: 16.[27] By physically expressing our doxology of gratitude, we profess to the world that in and through the resurrected Christ, we have access to heaven here on earth as we loudly acknowledge and proclaim the gracious presence of God in us.

> Regardless of life's challenges and threats and the daunting mountains confronting us, we should not grumble, complain or lose hope; rather, we should be filled with praise, transforming the situations into reasons for engaging in the doxology of gratitude.

When we perform this doxology of gratitude in the very nature and presence of God as people who have been called by the gospel to *"share in the glory of our Lord Jesus Christ,"*[28] we become glorified as we glorify God. As we perform our doxology of gratitude, we forget ourselves and focus on doing God's will, preparing for eternity. When our lifestyle becomes a doxology of gratitude, the hope of gratitude as an eschatological reality is born. What then is gratitude as an eschatological reality?

Endnotes

1 Alistair Begg, Made for His Pleasure: Ten Marks of a Vital Faith (United States: Moody Press, 1996) p. 125.

2 Psalm 86: 12

3 Donald S. Whitney, Spiritual Disciplines for the Christian Life (Colorado Springs: Navpress, 1991) p. 119.

4 John 1: 14 – "And the Word was made flesh, and dwelt among us, (and we beheld his glory, the glory as of the only begotten of the Father,) full of grace and truth."

5 Psalm 46: 1 – "God is our refuge and strength, A[a] very present help in trouble."

6 Revelation 4: 10–11 – "10 the twenty-four elders fall down before Him who sits on the throne and worship Him who lives forever and ever, and cast their crowns before the throne, saying: 11 'You are worthy, [a]O Lord, To receive glory and honour and power; For You created all things, And by Your will they [b]exist and were created'."

7 In Latin, *Gloria in Excelsis Deo*, "Glory in the highest to God," and in English, "Glory be to God on high."

8 Luke 2: 14 – "Glory to God in the highest, And on earth peace, goodwill[a] toward men!"

9 1 Peter 2: 9 – "But you are a chosen generation, a royal priesthood, a holy nation, His own special people, that you may proclaim the praises of Him who called you out of darkness into His marvellous light."

10 John 14: 15 – 15 "If you love Me, [d]keep My commandments."

11 John 14: 23 – "Jesus answered and said to him, 'If anyone loves Me, he will keep My word; and My Father will love him, and We will come to him and make Our home with him'."

12

13 "36 Master, which is the great commandment in the law? 37 Jesus said unto him, Thou shalt love the Lord thy God with all thy heart, and with all thy soul, and with all thy mind. 38 This is the first and great commandment. 39 And the second is like unto it, Thou shalt love thy neighbour as thyself.

40 On these two commandments hang all the law and the prophets."

14 Genesis 22

15 Abraham believing God implies that he accepted God's plan and word and responded to it by living a life of gratitude that God could love him this much. His acceptance of God's grace made him endure and follow God's instructions, with obedience in faith – act of gratitude, a living doxology. To unveil gratitude, we must die to the flesh – the circumstance and our desire and hold unto God's will, Word and way. Biblical gratitude cannot be separated from obedience and faith in God, as these are the pillars to true worship, which the Fathers seeks (John 4: 23).

16 Genesis 15: 6 – "And he believed in the Lord, and He accounted it to him for righteousness."

17 Psalm 27: 14 – "Wait on the Lord: be of good courage, and he shall strengthen thine heart: wait, I say, on the Lord."

18 Situation ethics is the position that moral decision-making is contextual or dependent on a set of circumstances – Sandra B. Rosenthal, "Situation ethics" – https: //www.britannica.com/topic/situation-ethics

19 By faith, Abel offered unto God a better sacrifice than Cain, by which Abel obtained witness that he was righteous, God testifying of his gifts: and by it he being dead yet speaketh.

20 Cain offered his first-fruits, which God Himself demanded from the people as offering (Deuteronomy 26: 2). In expressing our doxology of gratitude, we give to the Lord our first and best immediately because delayed obedience is disobedience. Cain gave his offerings at the end of the days, after several days, when he believed he had more than enough, indicating a lack of faith. God expects us to give to Him first, whether we have enough to eat or not, like Elijah instructed the widow to serve him first out of her nothing. As she obeyed in faith immediately, she received an overflow. In every situation, God wants us to have faith in Him and trust Him. Our expressed and instant obedience is the act of expressing gratitude, which is God's will for us – "In everything give thanks: for this is the will of God in Christ Jesus concerning you" (1 Thessalonians 5).

21 Malachi 1: 8 – "8 And if ye offer the blind for sacrifice, is it not evil? And if ye offer the lame and sick, is it not evil? Offer it now unto thy governor; will he be pleased with thee, or accept thy person? saith the Lord of hosts."

22 Peter Brunner, Worship in the Name of Jesus; tr M. H. Bertram; (Concordia: St Louis, 1968), p. 210.

23 Isaiah 38: 18–20 – "18 For the grave cannot praise thee, death cannot celebrate thee: they that go down into the pit cannot hope for thy truth. 19 The living, the living, he shall praise thee, as I do this day: the father to the children shall make known thy truth. 20 The Lord was ready to save me: therefore we will sing my songs to the stringed instruments all the days of our life in the house of the Lord."

24 Psalm 29 – "Give unto the Lord, O ye mighty, give unto the Lord glory and strength. 2 Give unto the Lord the glory due unto

his name; worship the Lord in the beauty of holiness.3 The voice of the Lord is upon the waters: the God of glory thundereth: the Lord is upon many waters.4 The voice of the Lord is powerful; the voice of the Lord is full of majesty..."

25 Eric Peterson, The Angels and the Liturgy; tr. R. Walls; (Darton, Longmann & Todd: London, 1964), p. 21.

26 2 Corinthians 4: 10 – "Always bearing about in the body the dying of the Lord Jesus, that the life also of Jesus might be made manifest in our body."

27 1 Timothy 3: 16 – "And without controversy great is the mystery of godliness: God was manifest in the flesh, justified in the Spirit, seen of angels, preached unto the Gentiles, believed on in the world, received up into glory."

28 2 Thessalonians 2: 14 – "Whereunto he called you by our gospel, to the obtaining of the glory of our Lord Jesus Christ."

Chapter Seven

Gratitude: An Eschatological Reality

As Christians, we live our lives based on our faith. Our moral reality is based on our faith, which comes from Jesus Christ. Every true Christian's moral reality of life should be, from Christ's perspective, their faith. Gratitude must be expounded in such a way that its starting point is Jesus Christ, as He, as the Son of God, has fulfilled the complete will of the Father for our living.

> It is difficult to visualise our God given greatness without gratitude. Gratitude is an unusual transfiguring power that transforms lives to experience God's goodness for both benefactor and beneficiary.

When we talk about gratitude, we are talking about living in perpetual joy because of the finished works of God through Jesus Christ that enable us to live our life in abundance. The eschatological reality of gratitude brings to mind that gratitude plays a key role in entering God's Kingdom,[1] as only those who abide by the will of God will enter God's Kingdom.[2] The signification of gratitude is that it is the commanded and expressed will of God[3] and a lifestyle in heaven; only the thankful can be true worshippers to join the heavenly choir. Jesus Christ is the complete and concrete eschatological reality, in the sense that He is the end of our morals and ethics of gratitude. Only the grateful worships the Lord in truth and *spirit* and God seeks[4] such people to be amongst the angels worshipping in paradise.[5,6] I am not saying that just thanking God or expressing gratitude qualifies you to enter God's kingdom. I am only trying to establish that entering God's Kingdom involves living a life of gratitude, which entails the process of acknowledging grace, accepting grace and responding to grace. It only takes a grateful heart to perform these actions. Nevertheless, it is imperative to understand that we are not qualified by our own effort and right to meet God's standard of holiness; none of us are good enough.[7] However, Jesus is, so through Him, we can enter heaven by accepting and responding to Him with a grateful heart. Jesus' suffering and the Eucharistic sacrifice of His life for us have given us the internal strength to abide by God's will and be thankful in all situations.[8]

The eschatological reality of gratitude seeks to explain that God's will is manifested in a two-fold manner: (1) Love Him and our neighbours.[9] Fulfilling this will requires possessing a clean heart;[10] a heart filled with appreciation and gratefulness, without which loving God and others and then attaining heaven are impossible, which are our ultimate heavenly purposes. You cannot love who you do not value; you can value and love only those who you appreciate. (2) Giving adoration in "spirit" and in "truth"[11] to God, which He demands and expects from us.[12] Thus, to unveil gratitude, gratitude must flow from a heart of freedom, a heart set free by "spirit and truth"[13] to inculcate in our body the potency and reality of gratitude in spirit and truth,[14] as the twenty-four elders do in heaven.[15]

> Worship is recognising, accepting and responding to grace, which empower us to see the Light of God, as it is for us to unveil gratitude for others to worship God.

The concept of acknowledging, accepting and responding to grace is born of the Spirit or work of the Spirit. People like Job and Daniel acknowledged, accepted and responded to grace, which empowered them to live in thanksgiving, despite the circumstances they faced. Thus, the eschatological reality of gratitude does not speak about just mere gratitude but divine gratitude,[16] encapsulated in the whole process of redemption. Here, allow me to ask you a question: If we are not divinely grateful on earth, how can we be of gratitude to worship in heaven?

Regarding the eschatological reality of gratitude, from Jesus' encounter with the ten lepers, it is evident that gratitude is an eschatological reality of heaven residency, where Jesus attested to the one who returned to give glory to God. Jesus was very concerned. The Scriptures, rather the gospels, indicate Jesus is not seemly to take record of attendance. However, on the occasion of healing the ten lepers, Jesus did, as He asked, *"Where are the nine?"*[17] It takes a thinker to be a *thanker*. Only those who take stock or can recount God's goodness upon their lives (thinker) can truthfully be grateful, thankful and appreciative (thanker) to live a life of gratitude. Gratitude as a command is concerned with the regenerated mind, which has a form and significance for our living on earth as ambassadors of Christ. God giving us His gift of grace and us accepting and responding to His gift have placed us in a covenanted relationship with Him bound by the command – *be thankful in all situations.* The eschatological reality of gratitude exposes us to living life according to the righteousness of God, as we cannot live in sin and still claim acceptance and respond to grace.[18] Our conduct of accepting God's gift of grace is measured by gratitude.

> Grace is not our property and cannot be manoeuvred as we chose; rather, it is a gift of God to make us what we can never be by receiving it in its form and essence as willed by God.

The eschatological reality of gratitude is seen and noted in God's amazing grace working gratuitously in our lives so that we can also respond gratuitously by loving others like ourselves.[19, 20] The reward for such compliance is never received on earth but in heaven.[21] Unless gratitude is unveiled, fully understanding what it means is impossible. Love and gratitude work together, as we cannot express gratitude without love, and gratitude can never be truly expressed to God or man without love. The spirit of gratitude imputes in us a conduct of the Kingdom – being thankful in every situation, which invariably is the law, conduct, theme and culture of God's Kingdom. The reality of gratitude is that it unites us with God's purpose and internalises in us the final unity to encounter Christ on the last day.

In conclusion, God's instructions are always our means of deliverance and freedom to inherit our heavenly blessings and live in unity with Him. Gratitude is one such instruction or command. In view of this, the eschatological reality of gratitude is not only fundamentally living a life of celebration of the grace of God freely given to us but also a command for our release into action, to be His sons and daughters.[22] Let me emphasise here and, at the same time, warn you that being Christian is not an exemption certificate that you will not face the challenges of life or simply can do anything and, therefore, jest with God. Gratitude in its reality gives us the full understanding of God's sovereignty that He does things as He pleases[23] and that no one can query Him.[24] Gratitude gives us the sense to respect, fear and *honour* God and not to play with or attempt to make Him our mate. Remember, gratitude is characterised by a free and gladsome action than spans the entirety of our human existence.

> Gratitude is the destroyer of I-ness that only recognises the self by opposing the sovereignty of the Trinity.

Unveiling gratitude, which will qualify us to be a worshipper both on earth and in heaven, entails possessing the essential features of Christ. These features are recognising, accepting and responding to grace.[25] When we are rooted and grounded in the grace of God, our gratitude potency intensifies and amplifies with our spiritual, intellectual and emotional appreciation.[26] Gratitude increases our spiritual awareness. Therefore, gratitude is fundamental to our spiritual life, as it creates the sensitivity in us to be highly aware of our boundaries and the need to rely on God and appreciate others.

Dr Mark Amadi

A Peculiar Eschatological Reality Phenomenon

Gratitude is an eschatological reality in that eternity is the home of those who respond to grace with gratitude, those who do the *will* of God. Right from the time God created us, we are bound to live the life of praise and thanksgiving.[27] God's intention for us is not to be priests and peculiar people only on earth but till eternity. Having been bestowed with such great grace, God expects us to practise and live a life of gratitude, which is an eschatological reality of our heavenly assignment as worshippers when we appear unto Him in eternity.

> *So come, let us sing unto the Lord: let us make a joyful noise to the rock of our salvation. 2 Let us come before his presence with thanksgiving, and make a joyful noise unto him with psalms. 3 For the Lord is a great God, and a great King above all gods. (Psalm 95: 1–3)*

Concerning gratitude as an eschatological reality, from the beginning of time, which started with Abraham,[28] God has been building His eternal worshippers (thankers); the undertaking began when He called out Israel and granted them tremendous unmerited privilege, showing them great favour above all other people (Deuteronomy 26: 19).[29] Deuteronomy 26: 19 reveals that each of God's blessings to us is for us to praise Him, making us holy people unto Him. From my experience in ministry, I have come to the revelation that Jehovah El-Olam (Genesis 21: 33) – the everlasting God – does everything for us (*whether we see it as good or bad* – Romans 8:28) to praise Him, which invariably crucifies our flesh and draws us closer to Him for dwelling in the fullness of His glory and abundance and bringing other people to Him by the reason of our thankfulness.

For example, Isaac, while waiting on God and enduring the labour of his faith in thanksgiving, was able to evangelise others[30] because of his attitude of gratitude (Genesis 26: 24-33). Thanking God in all circumstances blesses us with the hope that God will deliver us from those circumstances. It also helps us shift our focus from ourselves and our circumstances unto God, in whose presence we are always comforted, as was the case with Isaac. Thanking God in advance is the expression of our faith in God, and faith always pleases God.

Thanksgiving and gratitude are the perquisites for achieving eternity or eternal life, as upon them unveil our faith, trust, love and obedience to God:

> *18 For the wrath of God is revealed from heaven against all ungodliness and unrighteousness of men, who hold the truth in unrighteousness; 19 Because that which may be known of God is manifest in them; for God hath shewed it unto them. 20 For the invisible things of him from the creation of the world are clearly seen, being understood by the things that are made, even his eternal power and Godhead; so that they are without excuse: 21 Because that, when they knew God, they glorified him not as God, neither were thankful; but became vain in their imaginations, and their foolish heart was darkened. (Romans 1: 18 - 21)*

In God's eschatological plan of eternity, all who have accepted Him as their Lord and Saviour[31] become the eschatological Israelites, the chosen race by the Lord above all people upon the face of the earth (Deuteronomy 7: 6). More so, God made the Israelites a royal priesthood (Exodus 19: 6) – kingdom of priests – to offer sacrifice, gratitude and thanksgiving to Him in the form of worship. God engaged in such an act of peculiarity or particularism towards the Israelites for them to perform sacrifice for Him – to worship[32] Him as their King and Father, thereby making them royalty.

Salvational Grace

Gratitude, as an eschatological reality, is "thanks in eternity," God's ultimate end plan for His "royals and priests":[33]

Dr Mark Amadi

11 And all the angels stood round about the throne, and about the elders and the four beasts, and fell before the throne on their faces, and worshipped God, 12 Saying, Amen: Blessing, and glory, and wisdom, and thanksgiving, and honour, and power, and might, be unto our God for ever and ever. Amen. (Revelation 7: 11–12)

God is sovereign and worthy of all praise and thanksgiving. When we give thanks, we acknowledge His supremacy and goodness and appreciate Him for His grace upon us. Gratitude is accepting and responding to grace for the purpose of grace, to reign with Christ and to lead others to God's Kingdom to partake in the "thanks in eternity" (Revelation 17: 11–12). Gratitude as an eschatological reality speaks about us obeying God in all circumstances, not only appreciating God's benevolence but also enduring in all situations so that other people who are yet to know God can, owing to our attitude of gratitude, also praise and glorify God and seek Him in truth (1 Peter 2: 12).[34]

God created us to praise Him just as the angels in heaven before the foundation of the world (Job 38: 4–7). God designed us to be a people of praise and thanksgiving, unveiling gratitude. Since the advent of life on earth, God chose us and provided for us by giving us His grace through Christ for us to praise Him (Isaiah 43: 21). In Him we have obtained an inheritance, being predestinated according to His purpose and will for the praise of His glory through Christ (Ephesians 1: 11–12). God bought us with a price so that we might glorify Him in our body and in our spirit, which are His (1 Corinthians 6: 20). This unmerited favour binds us to live a life of gratitude, (2 Corinthians 4: 15).[35]

Paul enlightened us that the abounding grace we receive from God has favoured and enriched us beyond measures, and this grace has been designed purposely for our "sake" to promote our salvation to achieve eternal purpose, praising God in the heaven (2 Corinthians 4: 15). Also, through our act of thanksgiving for God's overflowing grace received, gratitude should abound to God so that by our gratitudinal expression, many may be led to praise God touched by our attitude of gratitude in all circumstances.

The lifestyle of every Christian should be such that they ceaselessly give thanks to God. Giving thanks and living a lifestyle of gratitude in all circumstances, as commanded by God, are objects of the labour of faith. We should labour so that as many as possible may see Christ through our attitude and be led to praise God and thank God till eternity, joining the royal priest and peculiar people in heaven to praise God. Our act of gratitude should always be for the glory of God.

> Gratitude is unveiled when it redounds to the glory of God, giving God increased praise so that His glory in the salvation of other people may abound.

I strongly believe that unveiling gratitude is an evangelical tool for winning as many souls to join in the "thanks in heaven" (Revelation 7: 11–12). Heaven or paradise or a place of eternity is the heavenly arena of unceasing worship and unending doxology, giving glory to God in the highest. Therefore, joining this "thanks in heaven" begins from here on earth where we are asked to be the salt and the light and to shine (Matthew 5: 13–16). Until our gratitude prompts others to seek God, our light will be yet to shine in the darkness of this world and our salt yet to enhance the flavour of life in this world for enabling them to join the "thanks in heaven" redemptive worship.

Eschatological Reality of Redemptive Worship (Thanks in Heaven)

The eschatological reality of redemptive worship begins with us living a life of gratitude here on earth, declaring God's praise and not our own praise. Pure gratitude leads us in redemptive worship that we are made to not only experience but also be a partaker in heaven.

Our act of gratitude here on earth prepares us for our heavenly task – joining the angelic singers and worshippers in heaven to worship the Lord as described in Revelation 7: 11–12. God's main purpose of creating us is to worship and praise Him. Praising or worshipping God is not just tied to the numerous blessings we have or have not received from God, but to His *intent* – to worship Him in all circumstances.

Put explicitly in terms of eschatological reality, redemptive worship is not based on God's benevolence of daily supplies and defence but our own love for Him, which is only expressed through the act of thanksgiving, being unveiled through a lifestyle of gratitude, living a life of the crucified Christ. The eschatological reality of gratitude, which results in redemptive worship, is never carnally minded but spiritual, originating from the spirituality of Christ that dwells in us to behold the Father's face on the last day (eternity). This is to unvaryingly say that without a thankful heart (*clean and pure*), the true expression of gratitude – a criterion for redemptive worship – is impossible.

The eschatological reality of gratitude as seen in the redemptive angelic worship in the Book of Revelation indicates that despite having no trace of sin, the worshippers were completely filled with utter humility before God almighty. I want to draw your attention here to the fact that the eschatological reality of gratitude is embedded and rooted in Christ-like humility, and to be of this reality, we must be humble in all our given benefits and positions, wealth and riches, professions and gifts (Philippians 2: 5–1).

Being of the mind of Christ prepares us to look inward to examine our faith and love for God. This reality makes us understand that a reality exists ahead of us that will be a determinant of joining the "thanks in heaven." True gratitude is the outburst of humility. As magnificent as we may picture the angels to be, they regard themselves as insignificant before God. It is, therefore, important to truly understand that true worship takes place in an atmosphere of humility, a broken and contrite heart, a deep sense of reverence.[36] Gratitude as an act of worship ought to characterise our whole lives and should not be limited to just on a Sunday or when something good happens to us.

> While thankfulness is the genesis of gratitude, gratitude is the revelation of thankfulness. As thankfulness is verbalised, gratitude becomes an endless demonstration of the revelation that thanksgiving can only verbalise.

The Book of Revelation makes this evident. The angels in heaven are engaged in the redemptive worship of God, owing to the Lamb's redemptive work. Some encircle the throne and sing melodiously : *"Worthy is the Lamb who was slain, to receive power and riches and wisdom and strength and honour and glory and blessing."*[37] Others splendidly praise the Lord: *"Amen! Blessing and glory and wisdom, Thanksgiving and honour and power and might, Be to our God forever and ever. Amen.*[38]*"* More so, in redemptive worship, another set of angelic worshippers luminously chant: *"…having a golden censer, came and stood at the altar. He was given much incense that he should offer it with the prayers of all the saints upon the golden altar which was before the throne.*[39]*"*

Concerning the qualification for redemptive worship, as mentioned above, the angels do not have even a trace of sin in them. They are perfect for the duty. Despite their exemplary perfection and position in heaven, they perform their duty with a sense of utter humility before God almighty, worshipping Him in humility.

The picture of redemptive worship is so awesome that we must build its replica here on earth through loving the Father and not getting carried away by His received blessings and miracles He gives us the grace to enact. All we do must be done in His name, giving Him all glory, without taking away any of His glory due to His name. In essence, regardless of how well God has blessed us, how great we have performed with the ability and gift God has given us like Prophet Elijah and how we consider ourselves humble and nice, if we, in any way, attempt to secure a share of God's glory, we lack thankfulness and shall unveil no gratitude, as behind our faces lies deceit and at the bedrock of our heart lies evil. No matter how successful you become, remember to give all the glory to God, as He has warned, *"I am the Lord: that is my name: and my glory will I not give to another, neither my praise to graven images[40]."*

> Holiness is not a theory test but a practical test, which question in the exponential (e) of thanksgiving raised to power infinity, to obtain gratitude for redemptive worship.

Therefore, to fit into the eschatological reality of the "reality of eternity," we must ensure that our act of gratitude enthrals God's holiness, coming to the knowledge and realisation that God's holiness incorporates all His attributes, for which we should be grateful and thankful. For examples, the attributes of God's holiness for which we should be thankful are loving kindness (Psalm 36: 7–9), compassion (Psalm 103: 8), forgiveness (Micah 7: 18–19), faithfulness (Deuteronomy 7: 9), justice (Isaiah 30: 18), mercy (Psalm 86: 15), graciousness (Psalm 86: 15) and many others.

To be of gratitude, in our lifestyle (worship), we should enhance our appreciation for God's holiness and our reverence for Him, and anything that diminishes or separates us from this reality of awe before His holiness should be eliminated mercilessly from our lifestyle (worship)[41] to unveil gratitude, an eschatological reality.

In eternity, we will be so overflowing in gratitude that it will stream out of our mouths uncontrollably. Therefore, to unveil gratitude, we should be filled with praise and thanksgiving always because God loves us, and He did so even before the creation of this world. His forgiveness and sustaining grace are major blessings for which we must be thankful. To qualify and join the heavenly angelic singers and worshippers, we must follow *verbatim* the instruction of the Bible – to be thankful in all circumstances (1 Thessalonians 5: 18).

Endnotes

1 Matthew 7: 21 – "Not everyone who says to Me, 'Lord, Lord,' shall enter the kingdom of heaven, but he who does the will of My Father in heaven."

2 Matthew 7: 21

3 1 Thessalonians 5: 18 – "In everything give thanks, for this is the will of God in Christ Jesus concerning you."

4 John 4: 23 – "But the hour is coming, and now is when the true worshipers will worship the Father in spirit and truth; for the Father is seeking such to worship Him."

5 Revelation 19: 5–7 – "5 Then a voice came from the throne, saying, 'Praise our God, all you His servants and those who fear Him, both[a] small and great!' 6 And I heard, as it were, the voice of a great multitude, as the sound of many waters and as the sound of mighty thunderings, saying, 'Alleluia! For the[b] Lord God Omnipotent reigns!' 7 Let us be glad and rejoice and give Him glory, for the marriage of the Lamb has come, and His wife has made herself ready."

6 Revelation 4: 6–11 – "6 – Before the throne there [a]was a sea of glass, like crystal. And in the midst of the throne, and around the throne, were four living creatures full of eyes in front and in back. 7 The first living creature was like a lion, the second living creature like a calf, the third living creature had a face like a man, and the fourth living creature was like a flying eagle. 8 The four living creatures, each having six wings, were full of eyes around and within. And they do not rest day or night, saying: 'Holy,[b] holy, holy, Lord God Almighty, Who was and is and is to come!' 9 Whenever the living creatures give glory and honour and thanks to Him who sits on the throne, who lives forever and

ever, 10 the twenty-four elders fall down before Him who sits on the throne and worship Him who lives forever and ever, and cast their crowns before the throne, saying:11 'You are worthy, [c]O Lord, To receive glory and honour and power; For You created all things, And by Your will they [d]exist and were created'."

7 1 Corinthians 6: 9–11 – "9 Do you not know that the unrighteous will not inherit the kingdom of God? Do not be deceived. Neither fornicators, nor idolaters, nor adulterers, nor [a]homosexuals, nor [b]sodomites, 10 nor thieves, nor covetous, nor drunkards, nor revellers, nor extortioners will inherit the kingdom of God. 11 And such were some of you. But you were washed, but you were [c]sanctified, but you were justified in the name of the Lord Jesus and by the Spirit of our God."

8 1 Thessalonians 5: 18 – "In everything give thanks: for this is the will of God in Christ Jesus concerning you."

9 Luke 10: 27 – "So he answered and said, 'You shall love the Lord your God with all your heart, with all your soul, with all your strength, and with all your mind,' and 'your neighbour as yourself'."

10 Psalm 24: 3–6

11 John 4: 23 – "But the hour is coming, and now is, when the true worshipers will worship the Father in spirit and truth; for the Father is seeking such to worship Him."

12 1 Thessalonians 5: 18

13 John 8: 36

14 John 4: 23

15 Revelation 4: 10

16 Divine gratitude here means gratitude born out of a pure and contrite heart.

17 Luke 17: 17 – "So Jesus answered and said, 'Were there not ten cleansed? But where are the nine?'"

18 Romans 6: 1–4 – "What shall we say then? Shall we continue in sin that grace may abound? 2 Certainly not! How shall we who died to sin live any longer in it? 3 Or do you not know that as many of us as were baptized into Christ Jesus were baptised into His death? 4 Therefore we were buried with Him through baptism into death, that just as Christ was raised from the dead by the glory of the Father even so we also should walk in newness of life."

19 Matthew 10: 8 – "Heal the sick, [a]cleanse the lepers, [b]raise the dead, cast out demons. Freely you have received, freely give."

20 Luke 14: 12–14 – "12 Then He also said to him who invited Him, "When you give a dinner or a supper, do not ask your friends, your brothers, your relatives, nor rich neighbours, lest they also invite you back, and you be repaid. 13 But when you give a feast, invite the poor, the [a]maimed, the lame, the blind. 14 And you will be blessed, because they cannot repay you; for you shall be repaid at the resurrection of the just."

21 Luke 6: 23 – "Rejoice in that day and leap for joy! For indeed your reward is great in heaven, for in like manner their fathers did to the prophets."

22 2 Corinthians 6: 18 – "I will be a Father to you, and you shall be my sons and daughters, Says the Lord Almighty."

23 Psalm 15: 3 – "But our God is in heaven; He does whatever He pleases."

24 Romans 9: 19

25 John 3: 14–16 – "14 And as Moses lifted up the serpent in the wilderness, even so must the Son of Man be lifted up, 15 that whoever believes in Him should [a]not perish but have eternal life. 16 For God so loved the world that He gave His only begotten Son, that whoever believes in Him should not perish but have everlasting life."

26 Colossians 2: 6–7 – "6 As you therefore have received Christ Jesus the Lord, so walk in Him, 7 rooted and built up in Him and established in the faith, as you have been taught, abounding [a]in it with thanksgiving."

27 1 Peter 2: 9–10 – "9 But ye are a chosen generation, a royal priesthood, an holy nation, a peculiar people; that ye should shew forth the praises of him who hath called you out of darkness into his marvellous light; 10 Which in time past were not a people, but are now the people of God: which had not obtained mercy, but now have obtained mercy."

28 Genesis 12: 1–3 – "Now the Lord had said unto Abram, Get thee out of thy country, and from thy kindred, and from thy father's house, unto a land that I will shew thee:2 And I will make of thee a great nation, and I will bless thee, and make thy name great; and thou shalt be a blessing:3 And I will bless them that bless thee, and curse him that curseth thee: and in thee shall all families of the earth be blessed."

29 Deuteronomy 26: 19 – "And to make thee high above all nations which he hath made, in praise, and in name, and in honour; and that thou mayest be an holy people unto the Lord thy God, as he hath spoken."

30 Genesis 26: 26 – "Then Abimelech went to him from Gerar, and Ahuzzath one of his friends, and Phichol the chief captain of his army."

31 Living a life of gratitude

32 Sacrifice here means giving praises to God. Giving praise to God means showing gratitude, which involves loving God, having faith in Him and living in obedience to His Word or instruction. Gratitude, as sacrifice, is far beyond uttering verbal expressions or raising hands in worship or shedding tears. It is a spiritual commitment in truth to God. When gratitude is unveiled through our lifestyle, the world sees God through us and reflects on who He is, seeking to know Him like Nicodemus who was moved by Jesus' teachings (John 3).

33 1 Peter 2: 9–10 – "9 But ye are a chosen generation, a royal priesthood, an holy nation, a peculiar people; that ye should shew forth the praises of him who hath called you out of darkness into his marvellous light; 10 Which in time past were not a people, but are now the people of God: which had not obtained mercy, but now have obtained mercy."

34 1 Peter 2: 12 – 12 "Having your conversation honest among the Gentiles: that, whereas they speak against you as evildoers, they may by your good works, which they shall behold, glorify God in the day of visitation."

35 2 Corinthians 4: 15 – "15 For all things are for your sakes, that the abundant grace might through the thanksgiving of many redound to the glory of God."

36 Isaiah 6: 3 – "And one cried unto another, and said, Holy, holy, holy, is the Lord of hosts: the whole earth is full of his glory." Also, see Revelation 4

37 Revelation 5: 12

38 Revelation 7: 12

39 Revelation 8: 3

40 Isaiah 42: 8

41 Romans 8: 35–39 – "Who shall separate us from the love of Christ? shall tribulation, or distress, or persecution, or famine, or nakedness, or peril, or sword? 36 As it is written, For thy sake we are killed all the day long; we are accounted as sheep for the slaughter. 37 Nay, in all these things we are more than conquerors through him that loved us. 38 For I am persuaded, that neither death, nor life, nor angels, nor principalities, nor powers, nor things present, nor things to come, 39 Nor height, nor depth, nor any other creature, shall be able to separate us from the love of God, which is in Christ Jesus our Lord."

Chapter Eight

Conclusion

Gratitude springs to life at the inception of awareness and understanding, and it goes far beyond our rosy emotional responses or special thanks for something we have done or received. Gratitude is the ever-evolving and expanding appreciation of God's grace – His presence and power, His sovereignty and compassion, His love and provision. When we tread in this direction, we become mature, thus living a life full of gratitude.

Hence, I view gratitude as one of the hallmarks of the maturity of Christians. It has both energising and motivating characteristics. In my "school of wilderness," I understood through the Holy Spirit that gratitude symbolises the internalised realisation and appreciation of God's finished works in us and for us. The acknowledgement of this truth creates in us a sound mind[1] that can see everything in the light of God, thereby enabling us to be thankful in all situations.

This "sound mind"[2] enables one to sincerely and truthfully express and extend the gift of God, by being optimistic and giving hope to others. Thus, gratitude can be described as a dynamic hub connecting the understanding of receiving and the power of giving, as gratitude not only pertains to the favours received but also serves as a reciprocal act, wherein one benevolently gives back to the giver and/or others. Gratitude is ethereal, spiritual and transcendent. It serves as a response to the recognition and acceptance of God's divine grace.

Let me emphasise that just as gratitude is emotionalised, expressed, demonstrated and verbalised as an external phenomenon that brings joy in unseemly situations or circumstances, gratitude is also a choice – the outcome of one's core values and beliefs. Thus, it is important to understand here that our perception/perspective of life holds a belief about its context and/or purpose. Hence, if we walk with God's perspective, we can make gratitude a choice. David did so, giving thanks in every situation and circumstance, seeking God's heart. God saw him as a man who would stay true to His *will* – to be forever thankful.

> *And when He had removed him, He raised up for them David as king, to whom also He gave testimony and said, "I have found David the son of Jesse, a man after My own heart, who will do all My will." (Acts 13: 22)*

God instructed us that being thankful is His expressed *will*. It is now up to us to either accept or decline His will, according to 1 Thessalonians 5: 18. Our beliefs automatically set our expectations and shape our interpretation of the way we see and react to things. David did so from his belief of God being the ultimate one, deserving of praise and worship in all situations. Hence, he chose to be a worshipper of the living God whom he knew would always deliver him.

> Our life is an opportunity to behold the magnitude of God's greatness that unfolds every day in our lives, in diverse situations and circumstances, to make us the unique and wonderful person He has made us to be. If only we can recount and bring to record all His benefits we have received from time immemorial! Without being a thinker, we cannot be a thanker.

When gratitude is unveiled, it reveals our maturity in Christ Jesus, the Christ living in us, as we become humble, compassionate, thoughtful and purposeful, in alignment with God's *will*. Gratitude establishes a divine connection between God and us – an awareness and thankfulness of God's presence and benevolence towards us as well as others. It is the measuring tape of our maturity in Christ, as it also empowers us to live out God's will through our lifestyle.

Scientific studies have revealed that gratitude plays a key role in our well-being and mental health, and scientific evidence attesting to the contribution of gratitude to one's psychological and social well-being has been on the rise. Moreover, clinical trials suggest that the practice of gratitude is associated with improved health, such as lowered blood pressure, improved immune functions and well-being, reduced depression, anxiety and substance abuse.[3]

Likewise, gratitude interventions have been shown to function as a preventative measure in reducing bodily complaints, which helps in improving sleep duration and efficiency as well as mood and cardiovascular functioning.[4]

> Gratitude is humility in disguise, rooted in one's supernatural being, manifesting through the natural being, made known by acceptance, attention and responsibility.

The aforementioned quote explains that gratitude is spiritual, which manifests in the physical realm and dwells amongst men to build as well as strengthen relationships and unveil the nature of God to the natural man, to behold God's goodness through us – the grateful ones! The uniqueness of gratitude is that it helps us realise that all we have has been given have been free gifts from God and we have been created to give back to God[5] as well as our fellow beings.[6] Gratitude sets us free from guilt, as it empowers us to always be content in whichever situation we find ourselves. On a more personal note, I believe it is difficult for gratitude to exist where there is no freedom, as gratitude cannot be forced or demanded. Hence, it is a choice. For instance, when Jesus healed the ten lepers, He didn't force any of them to express their gratitude (though He expected it, as it is the will of God). However, out of their free will, nine of them decided not to be grateful.

Unveiling Gratitude

On the other hand, one returned out of his free will to express his gratitude.[7] Therefore, gratitude is a choice, and it must be born out of the "freedom of one's will," and I can say that this "freedom" symbolises spiritual empowerment – who the Son sets free is free indeed.[8]

> Hidden gratitude is no expression of gratitude and is never useful to anyone, not even to God.

The realisation that everything we have is a gift from God[9] sets us free from spiritual ingratitude wherein we look down on others, as God did not create anything or any person as insignificant, inferior, or purposeless. Therefore, gratitude is the defining factor required to fulfil a purpose, as we have been created on purpose and for a purpose. Hence, the lifestyle of gratitude is important in building our sense of interconnectedness, to fulfil the will of God. In fact, or perhaps, no perfect relationship can exist without the act of gratitude, as it entails focusing on others rather than the self.[10] Unveiling gratitude involves accepting God's grace and living and expressing God's love to all instead of self-promotion and self-aggrandisement. Gratitude cannot be unveiled until we experience the transforming power of God's grace in our lives, and until then, we remain enslaved by our greed, hurtfulness, ill habits and self-concern, which disconnect us from others.

To conclude, gratitude should not be reduced to just a feeling. From the beginning of time and in ancient religious scriptures and modern social science research, the virtue of gratitude has been endorsed as a necessary human characteristic with the capacity to make one's life better for oneself and for others. Gratitude is the loveliest of the virtues, as it does not only elevate a person but also edifies the person to whom it is directed. Cultivate a sense of gratitude, as it empowers you to unveil God to others and edifies them to know about God. Moreover, it keeps you joyful, helps you appreciate all things and keeps you prepared to always respond to God's grace, for now and for eternity.

Endnotes

1 For God has not given us a spirit of fear, but of power and of love and of a sound mind (2 Timothy 1: 7)

2 Ibid

3 , R. A. Emmons, Thanks! How the New Science of Gratitude Can Make You Happier (New York, NY: Houghton-Mifflin, 2007), pp. 12–34. Also see Emmons, 2013 as well as Emmons & McCullough, 2003.

4 R. A. Emmons, & McCullough, M. E., "Counting blessings versus burdens: An experimental investigation of gratitude and subjective well-being in daily life," Journal of Personality and Social Psychology, (2003, 84, 377–89. Also see Hill, P. L, Allemand, M., & Roberts, B. W., "Examining the pathways between gratitude and self-rated physical health across adulthood," Personality and Individual Differences, (2010, 54, 92–96).

5 Revelation 4: 11

6 Hebrews 6: 10

7 Luke 17: 11–19

8 John 8: 36

9 1 Chronicles 29: 14 "But who am I, and who are my people, that we should be able to offer so willingly as this? For all things come from You, and of Your own have we given You."

10 Philippians 2: 3

Bibliography

Birnbaum, T. H. & Friedman, H. H. "Gratitude and generosity: Two keys to success and happiness" (2014) viewed 15 February 2017, from papers.ssrn.com.

Bridges, J. Respectable Sins: Confronting the Sins We Tolerate (Colorado Springs, CO: Tyndale House, 2014).

Brunner, P. Worship in the Name of Jesus; tr. M. H. Bertram (St Louis, MO: Concordia, 1968).

Carmichael, L. Friendship: Interpreting Christian Love (London, UK: T & T Clark International, 2004).

Diessner, R., & Lewis, G. "Further validation of the gratitude, resentment, and appreciation test (GRAT)," The Journal of Social Psychology (2007, 147, 445–47).

Dockery, D. S., & David, E. G. Seeking the Kingdom (Wheaton, IL: Harold Shaw, 1992).

Dongsheng, J. W. Understanding Watchman Nee: Spirituality, Knowledge, and Formation (Eugene, OR: Wipf & Stock Pub, 2012).

Dubois, C. M, Beach, S. R., Kashdan, T.B., Nyer M. B., Park E.R., Celano C. M., Huffman J. C. "Positive psychological attributes and cardiac outcomes: associations, mechanisms, and interventions," Psychosomatics (2012, 53:303–18).

Emmons, R. A. "Is gratitude queen of the virtues and ingratitude king of the vices?" https://scottbarrykaufman.com/wp-content/uploads/2017/09/Emmons-paper-for-Gratitude-Complaint-consultation-September-2017.pdf

Emmons, R. A., & McCullough, M. E. (Eds.). The Psychology of Gratitude (New York, NY: Oxford University Press, 2004).

Emmons, Robert A. Thanks: How the New Science of Gratitude Can Make You Happier (Boston, MA: Houghton Mifflin, 2007).

Emmons, R. A., & Kneezel, T. T. "Giving thanks: Spiritual and religious correlates of gratitude," Journal of Psychology and Christianity (2005, 24(2), 140–48).

Emmons, R. A. Gratitude Works! A 21-Day Program for Creating Emotional Prosperity (San Francisco, CA: Jossey Bass, 2013).

Emmons, R. A., & Hill, J. Words of Gratitude: For Mind, Body, and Soul (Philadelphia, PA: Templeton Foundation Press, 2001).

Emmons, R. A., & McCullough, M. E. "Counting blessings versus burdens: An experimental investigation of gratitude and subjective well-being in daily life," Journal of Personality and Social Psychology, (2003, 84, 377–89).

Geraghty, A. W., Wood, A. M., & Hyland, M. E. "Dissociating the facets of hope: Agency and pathways predict dropout from unguided self-help therapy in opposite directions," Journal of Research in Personality, (2010, 44(1), 155–58).

Gerrish, B. A., Grace and Gratitude: The Eucharist Theology of John Calvin (Eugene, Oregon: Wipf & Stock: 1993).

Hill, P. L, Allemand, M., & Roberts, B. W. "Examining the pathways between gratitude and self-rated physical health across adulthood," Personality and Individual Differences (2010, 54, 92–96).

Huffman, J. C., Mastromauro, C. A., Boehm, J. K., Seabrook, R, Fricchione, G. L., Denninger, J. W., & Lyubomirsky S. "Development of a positive psychology intervention for patients with acute cardiovascular disease," Heart International (2011, 6: e14).

Kempis, T. A. The Imitation of Christ (London, UK: Penguin Classics, 2005).

Kleinig, J. "The mystery of doxology." https://www.doxology.us/wp-content/uploads/2015/03/52_The-Mystery-of-Doxology-by-John-Kleinig.pdf

Lau, P. H. W. Identity and Ethics in the Book of Ruth: A Social Identity Approach (Berlin, Germany: Walter de Gruyter & Co., 2010).

McCullough, M. E., Emmons, R. A., & Tsang, J. "The grateful disposition: A conceptual and empirical topography," Journal of Personality and Social Psychology (2002, 82, 112–27).

Mckay, B., & McKay, K. "The spiritual disciplines: Gratitude." https://www.artofmanliness.com/2017/12/18/spiritual-disciplines-gratitude/

Mills P. J., Redwine, L., Wilson, K., Pung, M. A., Chinh, K., Greenberg, B. H., Lunde, O., Maisel, A., Raisinghani, A., Wood, A., & Chopra, D. "The role of gratitude in spiritual well-being in asymptomatic heart failure patients. spirituality in clinical practice." PubMed (2015, 2: 5–17).

Peterson, C., & Seligman, M. E. Character Strengths and Virtues: A Classification and Handbook (New York, NY: Oxford University Press, 2004).

Peterson, E. The Angels and the Liturgy; tr. R. Walls; (London, UK: Darton, Longmann & Todd, 1964).

Rozanski, A. "Behavioral cardiology: current advances and future directions." Journal of the American College of Cardiology. (2014, 64: 100–10).

Sacco, S. J., Park C. L., Suresh D. P., Bliss, D. "Living with heart failure: Psychosocial resources, meaning, gratitude and well-being. Heart & lung," The Journal of Critical Care (2014, 43: 213–8).

Spurgeon, C. H. Commentary on Matthew: The Gospel of the Kingdom (London, UK: The Banner of Truth Trust, 2010).

Steindl-Rast, D. "Gratitude as thankfulness and as gratefulness." In R. A. Emmons and M. E. McCullough (Eds.), The Psychology of Gratitude (New York, NY: Oxford University Press, 2004), pp. 282–89.

Rosenthal, S. B. "Situation ethics." https://www.britannica.com/topic/situation-ethics

Thayer, J. F., Yamamoto, S. S., Brosschot, J. F. "The relationship of autonomic imbalance, heart rate variability and cardiovascular disease risk factors." International Journal of Cardiology (2010, 141: 122–31).

Trueblood, D. E. Essays in Gratitude (Nashville, TN: Broadman, 1982).

Tryon, E. The New Dictionary of Thoughts: A Cyclopedia of Quotations (Whitefish, MT: Literary Licensing, LLC, 2012).

Uhder, J. "The benefits of gratitude in spiritual formation: Collaborative of gratefulness in a Christian church community" (Doctor of Psychology (PsyD), 2016, Paper 193. P.2). http://digitalcommons.georgefox.edu/cgi/viewcontent.cgi?article=1192&context=psyd

Watkins, P. C. Gratitude and the Good Life: Toward A Psychology of Appreciation (New York, NY: Springer, 2014).

Wood, A. M., Froh, J. J., & Geraghty, A. A. "Gratitude and well-being: A review and theoretical integration," Clinical Psychology Review (2010, 30(7), 890–905).

Psychosom Med. Author manuscript; available in PMC 2017 Jul 1. Published in final edited form as: Psychosom Med. 2016 Jul-Aug; 78(6): 667–676. doi: 10.1097/PSY.0000000000000316 https://europepmc.org/articles/pmc4927423

About the Book

The message contained in this book is inspirationally written to enable readers understand and live in gratitude.

Coining the term "translational gratitude," Dr Mark conveys the pivotal idea that gratitude is not based on reciprocity but pure love. He seeks to unveil the gratitude that empowers us to express the divine nature of God as we interact with all of His creation, especially man.

Translational gratitude is not only expressed with words, it is reflected in character and attitude.

He explains how a heart of gratitude brings contentment, fortifies against sin, builds healthy relationships and fosters good health.

Finally, the book expounds on the doxology and eschatology of gratitude.

About the Author

Dr Mark Amadi, a prophet, is the Senior Pastor of the Fountain of Peace Ministries, based in London, UK. He is passionate about empowering lives and bringing the practical message of Christ's love to a hurting world. He is also the author of "Water of Life" – a Christian daily devotional circulated via print and electronic media across Europe, North America and Africa.

He is widely read and holds several educational qualifications and professional positions –BSc (Nigeria), MA, MSc, DBTS, PhD, and Cardiovascular Disease Researcher (UK). An associate of Christ Church University, Canterbury (UK) and a member of the "European Research Network on Global Pentecostalism" (GloPent).

He is also a practicing member of the British Association for Cardiovascular Prevention and Rehabilitation (BACPR), British Society of Allergy and Clinical Immunology (BSACI) and British Society for Heart Failure (BSH).

Index

A

Anthropomorphic 5

Attitude 4, 6, 12–13, 17, 28, 30, 35, 40, 48–49, 58, 62, 67, 69–70, 72–78, 85, 89, 95–97, 100, 105, 110, 114, 126, 128–129, 149

B

Behaviour 4, 28, 55, 72–73

Benevolence 3, 9–10, 40, 55, 58, 74, 89, 98, 128, 130, 141

C

Cardiovascular 57, 90, 142, 146, 148, 150

Character 1, 4, 6–7, 17, 26, 28, 32, 49, 54, 64, 110, 147, 149

Christ 2–9, 11–15, 19–21, 23, 25–26, 28, 30–37, 39, 41, 43–45, 48, 52, 58–60, 62–66, 68–72, 74–76, 78–81, 83, 85, 89, 92–97, 99–105, 107, 109–114, 116–117, 120–122, 124–125, 128–130, 134–137, 139, 141–142, 146, 150

Christ Jesus 3–4, 7, 9, 12, 15, 21, 23, 25, 28, 30–31, 35–37, 39, 41, 52, 60, 64–66, 68, 78, 80–81, 85, 101, 103, 105, 114, 120, 134–137, 139, 141

Christian life 57, 74, 76–78, 108, 118

Christians 4, 6, 70–71, 73, 100, 122, 140

Commandment 49–50, 65, 75, 105, 112–113, 119

Comparative gratitude 3, 41

Consequences of Discontentment 4, 86

Contentment 4, 50, 53, 56, 58, 82–87, 96, 100, 102, 112, 149

Contentment and Gratitude 4, 83, 85

Covetousness 4, 37, 48–52, 54, 64–65, 83, 85

Cross 3–5, 9, 12, 41, 59, 70–71, 76, 97, 102–103, 115

D

Dejection 35

Depression 35, 42, 57, 90, 142

Devourers 35

Disappointment 35

Discouragement 35, 108

Disease 35, 57, 59, 90–91, 109, 146, 148, 150

Doctrine 4, 10, 12, 61–62, 69–72, 79

Doxologicalise 98, 103

Doxology 4, 98, 103, 105–106, 111–112, 114–117, 119–120, 129, 147, 149

Doxology of gratitude 4, 98, 105, 111, 114–117, 120

E

Emotions 28, 48, 100, 112

Eschatological Reality 5, 13, 117, 122–130, 132

Eternity 3, 18, 96, 117, 126–130, 132, 143

Express 4, 6, 8, 10, 17–19, 22, 28, 32–34, 43, 45, 49, 53, 55, 68, 74, 77–78, 81, 94–95, 107, 112–114, 124, 140, 142–143, 149

Expression 9, 11, 17–18, 23, 27, 29–30, 33, 40, 42, 50, 53, 70, 82, 87, 92, 98, 103, 112–113, 116, 127, 129–130, 143

F

Faith 4–5, 14, 26, 30, 36, 38, 40, 43–44, 53, 56, 63, 70, 72–74, 77, 79, 91, 107–108, 110, 113–116, 118–120, 122, 126–127, 129–130, 137–138

G

God 1–41, 43–89, 91–144, 149

God's love 18, 25, 32–33, 86, 143

Grace 1–9, 12–27, 29, 31, 33, 35, 38, 40–41, 45–46, 51, 53–54, 58–63, 66–68, 70, 72–74, 81–83, 86, 95–99, 105, 107, 109–111, 113, 116, 118–119, 122–129, 131, 133, 136, 138, 140, 143, 146

Grateful 1–3, 9, 15, 17, 21–23, 31–33, 42–46, 48, 51–54, 58, 61–62, 68, 70–71, 74–77, 80, 82–83, 85, 89–90, 94–95, 97, 100, 107–110, 113, 122–124, 132, 142, 147

Gratitude 1–13, 15–36, 38–65, 67–98, 100–103, 105–117, 119–120, 122–133, 136–138, 140–149

Gratitudinal Thankfulness 4, 109

H

Heart 2, 4, 6, 9, 11–12, 17, 19, 21–28, 30–31, 33, 36, 38–39, 46–61, 65, 67, 71, 74–76, 78, 80–83, 86, 89–93, 97–98,

101, 108, 111–114, 119, 123, 127, 130–132, 135–136, 141, 146–150

Humility 4, 17, 23, 36, 39–41, 46, 50, 56, 58, 60, 69, 82–84, 86, 95, 97, 100, 103, 105–106, 130–131, 142

I

Ingratitude 12, 48, 54–55, 57, 73, 106, 108, 110, 112, 143, 145

K

Kingdom 11, 25, 36, 38–40, 63, 76, 92–93, 122, 124, 127–128, 134–135, 145, 148

M

Murmuring 4, 48, 52–57, 65

Mystery 3, 11, 23, 35–36, 39–40, 46, 61–63, 117, 121, 147

N

New nature 3–5

P

Parasympathetic 90

Particularism 127

Peculiarity 127

Potency of Gratitude 4, 49, 77–78, 81, 87–89

Pride 4, 24, 48, 57–61, 67, 92, 111

Psychology 28, 42, 44, 63–64, 144–148

Psychological 42, 61, 64, 72, 82, 90, 112, 142, 145

Pure heart 26, 28, 91–93, 113

Purity 4, 26, 91–93

R

Redemptive worship 5, 13, 129–132

S

Sin 4, 21, 24, 26, 33, 49–60, 65, 71, 83, 86, 89, 94, 106, 110–113, 115, 124, 130–131, 136, 149

Spirit 2–3, 5–6, 11, 18–20, 22–24, 34–37, 39–40, 43–44, 48, 50–57, 65, 67, 72–74, 76, 82, 86, 89–94, 96, 100, 102, 105, 108, 112, 114–115, 121–124, 128, 134–135, 140, 144

Spiritual Brokenness 3, 6

spiritual sacrifice 115

T

Thankers 126

Thankfulness 2, 4, 15, 54, 59, 69, 71, 97–98, 108–109, 111–114, 126, 131–132, 141, 148

Thanks in Heaven 5, 13, 129–130

Thanksgiving 4, 9, 12, 15–17, 19, 23, 27, 29, 35, 41, 43, 48–50, 55–57, 72, 75, 79, 88, 105, 110–111, 113–114, 123, 126–128, 130–133, 137–138

Translational gratitude 3, 32–34, 82, 149

U

Unthankfulness 54, 61, 112

Unveiling 1–4, 13, 40, 53, 57, 61–62, 93–94, 97–98, 102–103, 111, 113, 125, 128–129, 143

W

Worship 3, 5, 10, 12–13, 22–23, 27–28, 34, 41, 45–46, 51, 69–72, 75–78, 80, 82, 88, 92, 98, 106, 111–112, 118–121, 123, 127, 129–132, 134–135, 138, 141, 145

Worshippers 72, 79, 81, 122, 126, 130–131, 133

www.ingramcontent.com/pod-product-compliance
Lightning Source LLC
Chambersburg PA
CBHW021108080526
44587CB00010B/430